# GunDigest® Book of the
# TACTICAL RIFLE

## Patrick Sweeney

Published by

Gun Digest® Books, an imprint of F+W Media, Inc.
Krause Publications • 700 East State Street • Iola, WI 54990-0001
715-445-2214 • 888-457-2873
www.krausebooks.com

To order books or other products call toll-free 1-800-258-0929
or visit us online at www.krausebooks.com, www.gundigeststore.com
or www.Shop.Collect.com

Cover photo courtesy Yamil R. Sued/Photoworks, www.hotgunshots.com

ISBN-13: 978-1-4402-1432-5
ISBN-10: 1-4402-1432-8

Cover Design by Tom Nelsen
Designed by Kara Grundman
Edited by Dan Shideler

Printed in the Unites States of America

# Dedication

First of all, I'd like to dedicate this to all the faithful readers, those of you who have enjoyed previous volumes. Without your allegiance, my fun would not be so extensive, and my expanding base of knowledge greatly restricted.

As well, I'd like to give a nod to those who are not fans. Without feedback, authors (and radio broadcasters, movie stars and politicians) will veer off into areas they themselves enjoy, and leave their customers behind.

But through it all, the continuing credit goes to a deserving Felicia, who pointed out the path through the thickets, and patiently waited while I figured out how to hack through the metaphorical underbrush.

Have fun.

# Table of Contents

**Introduction** ..................................................... 7

**Chapter One:** Selection and Training ............................ 9

**Chapter Two:** Overview of Types ................................ 19

**Chapter Three:** The AK .........................................27

**Chapter Four:** The M14/M1A .................................... 43

**Chapter Five:** Bullpups .........................................63

**Chapter Six:** The Kel-Tec RFB ................................. 73

**Chapter Seven:** The Steyr AUG ................................. 81

**Chapter Eight:** The FN SCAR ...................................97

**Chapter Nine:** The FAL.........................................115

**Chapter Ten:** PDWs .............................................133

**Chapter Eleven:** Ammo.......................................... 149

**Chapter Twelve:** The SIG 556...................................161

**Chapter Thirteen:** Sniper Rifles ...............................171

**Chapter Fourteen:** Rimfires ................................... 193

**Chapter Fifteen:** Slings and Such.............................199

**Chapter Sixteen:** Reloading................................... 211

**Conclusion** ..................................................... 222

# Acknowledgments

First up, I'd like to thank Steve Hornady, of Hornady ammo, for the cartons of ammo he's sent me for this and other projects. Also, Jeff Hoffman of Black Hills has been a supporter of mine and other gun writers' efforts, such that we as a group could probably not do what we do without the support of those two gentlemen.

FNH-USA provided much in the way of guns, gear, ammo and access. Not only did they host me at their 3-gun match (with CMMG) but they sent me an invitation to a private, writers-only afternoon of shooting with the array of their new firearms, including the 40mm grenade launcher. Elaine and David Golladay were quite clear when they sent me the invite: "This is not for everyone you know." Clearly they know gun writers. There is usually a feeding frenzy when the ammo boxes are opened. To kick open cartons of practice 40mm grenades, in full view of gun writers, is to invite a riot.

Marc Christiansen of DS Arms was a very accommodating host, and not only saw that my excreble Indian FAL parts kit was ushered through the build process, but that whenever a problem came up, it was handled quickly and efficiently. As a result of that visit I gained a much greater understanding of the FAL than I had gotten in several decades of reading, and some shooting.

Marc Krebs is, well, a surpassingly gifted gunsmith, and an entertaining host. If you feel the AK is the rifle to have over all others, he should be on your short list to build you one or improve your current AK.

Century Arms has done what a lot of people said either couldn't be done, or felt was something far in the future, the all-USA made AK. Now that they've done it, I think we're going to see more USA-made AKs, and the world will be better for it. Plus, the folks at Century don't blanch when I send them photos of their firearms with dirt shoveled onto them, or dripping from the swamp-bath they've just received.

And, a tip of the hat to Kel-Tec, who do not just build excellent guns at an affordable price. They forge engineering and design progress that is often emulated by others. You may feel that their firearms are just a little too "industrial" looking for your tastes, but when it comes to performance in a particular package size, they are often the ones to look to first.

Finally, SIG. People tend to think of them as "those guys who made all the 226s for the Navy SEALS." In Europe, they are the rifle company who also makes handguns. They have been kind and generous in sending me product, and looking the other way while I heinously abuse their precision-built rifles.

So, get out there, handle the products you've read about, and see what fits you. Then buy one, or two, and train with it. Learning to shoot well is entertaining, a good way to keep sharp, focused and fit, and it is your right, heritage and duty as an American citizen.

*Patrick Sweeney*
*November 2010*

# Introduction

What is a tactical rifle? To many, it is something black, with rails and plastic and a big magazine. Something faintly sinister-looking. That might even be true in some cases, but it's a rather specialized example. A general description of a tactical rifle might be "a rifle suitable for fighting, either in combat, or personal defense, with the mechanical certainty and ruggedness that such conditions require."

"Tactical" might be something in a big cartridge, or a small one. You might find that the FN 5.7 is perfect for your needs at the moment, while someone else would find that only the .408 Chey-Tac would do. Tactical is as tactical does. Or needs.

For a member of the 7th Cavalry, dismounted and facing an uncertain future at Little Big Horn that June day in 1876, a tactical rifle would have been a Henry or a Spencer. On a certain October day in 1918, the bolt-action rifle wielded by Alvin York was a tactical rifle. Tactical is as tactical requires.

But you aren't here to argue the existential basis of a tactical rifle, nor the peculiar requirements of any given moment in time. No, you want to know about rifles that hold lots of bullets, or those that send a single one to a precise spot, a long, long way away. You want to know about ARs, and AKs, and FALs, and AUGs, and, well, there's just *something* about the rifles we are interested in. Face it, when you read the three-letter names of each of those rifles in the previous sentence, a photo of each flashed in your memory.

Good! That means you're hooked. I will, however, shy away from AR lust here. I've covered them extensively in several other books (and more on the way) so this is the time for the non-ARs to rise. We'll look at rifles that are available, and not ARs, or at least mostly not ARs. The Stoner system is known mostly for being ubiquitous, and thus inescapable.

We'll also delve a bit into how to use these very specialized rifles and what to feed them, since a rifle without skills or ammo is a sorry tool with which to try to solve a pressing problem. And throughout, I hope we'll have fun and learn stuff.

*Patrick Sweeney*
*October, 2010*

**CHAPTER 1**

# Selection and Training

Selecting a tactical rifle is easy. Go down to the gun shop. Look over the selection. See which ones are within your disposable income fund limits. Pick the one you like. There, easy, right? OK, OK, not particularly funny or helpful, but I'm trying to make a point here. Tactical is as tactical does. Do you need to be hitting targets with great gusto 1,000 yards away? Then the cute little short-barreled rifle (SBR) AR-15 in 5.56 is not going to be a particularly useful choice.

You have to know what you want, to be able to select what will work. You also have to know what you can do. If you can't take recoil, then the world's best rifle, chambered in .338 Lapua, or .408 Chey-Tac, is not going to work for you.

"What do you want?" It's a valid question, along with "What do you need? And where will you be using it?" As much as I dislike bullpups, were I getting into and out of vehicles all day long, I would certainly see the attraction. Any vehicle, standard sedan, SUV or Humvee is not fun when you're trying to maneuver an FAL through the door. So you have to select based on distance, obstacles, threat and target hardness and numbers.

Faced with a street full of zombies, I think I'd much rather have a tactical 10/22 than any AR in existence (unless it were a dedicated .22LR AR.) If the threat is going to be sniping at me from 600+ yards, I certainly would prefer not to be hampered with an M4, Something bigger, and with a better trigger, would be very nice right about then.

One absence you're bound to notice here is the AR itself. Since I've already pretty well covered the AR, I figured the last thing you'd want is more AR. Still, some of you may miss not having a Stoner-system rifle on these pages, so I did use one or two in photos to illustrate other ideas.

Why be so coy about offering a "best tactical rifle?" After all, is no lack of experts who will tell you which particular one (and with which options) you simply must have, or you lose your tacti-cool status and devolve to mall ninja. As I've pointed out before, if we were all the same size, clothing and boot manufacturers would only need to stock one size. And so it is with rifles.

If you need power, get it. If you can't stand recoil, don't let someone sell you on the benefits of a caliber bigger than you can stand. If you are not a reloader, don't fall for something in "the newest and best caliber, ever" that you'll have to reload for in order to have anything to shoot.

Keep in mind that once you have selected a particular rifle, you are not just buying the rifle, but you are buying the rifle system. I'm not using "system" as the latest over-used military procurement buzzword, but just to remind you that you are locked into that rifle. Let me give you an example: the AR-15. There's a reason it is popular, and part of that is ubiquity. It's everywhere. I just received a flier via email from a wholesale dealer that does retail internet sales. They are offering 20-round AR-15 magazines, your choice of color coating, for $6.95 each. Buy 10 and you get a price break. And you can find similar deals all the time, from a hundred different supplier. You'll find similar situations with respect to magazines for the AK (47 or 74) and the FAL (as long as you buy metric and not English), which is not always the case with other rifles.

Compare those to the last time I bought magazines for the Golani Sporter in the rack, the Century Arms rebuild of a Galil. The magazines cost $25 each, and one of the four required hand-fitting to lock in place. I have a couple of footlockers full of AR magazines accumulated over the years. I do not see my acquiring a similar number of Galil mags.

Add to that scope mounts, railed handguards, sling mounts and so on. You can find the "perfect" rifle, and find that you can't get anything to bolt onto it. Now, if you're a "iron sights are fine" shooter, and have no perceived need to mount a light or other stuff on your rifle, fine. But you're still going to have to find magazines and ammo. So it hardly matters how inexpensive a rifle may be, if ammo doesn't exist.

As long as you can get the extras for your rifle, don't let my or anyone else's personal opinions sway you. You want it? Go get it. Don't let the internet experts, the gun shop commandos or others divert you from your path. Have fun.

If you are buying something for competition (as well as defense or the coming zombie apocalypse) then pay attention to your scores. If you buy gear to improve your scores, and your scores don't improve, to steal a line from an advertising campaign and change it: "It may not be the shoes." Gear can only do so much, and money spent on gear is money not spent on practice ammo, training and match fees.

Now, one other aspect of buying tactical gear that will never cease to be controversial is: what cost? The tactical set at the local gun shop will tell you that if you do not have the exact item that SEALS/SOCOM/SF his brother-in-law uses, then you are some sort of in-

No rifle will shoot by itself, regardless of what the anti-gunners think. And unless you practice with it, none is as good as it could be.

Seek out instruction. Even bad instruction from which you learn what not to do, is better than none. And this day was good instruction.

ternet commando, an airsofter (with apologies to the airsoft set) and you shouldn't be seen on any respectable range with your low-rent gear.

An old adage that sums it up goes like this: "Buy cheap, buy again; buy quality, buy once." Which is true, but it leaves out a very important element of the buying quality: knowing what works best for you. Let's use as an example a scope. Now, the government buys expensive because performance matters. Getting an extra couple of minutes of daylight out of a quality scope can mean the difference between hitting or missing the high-value target the team was sent to whack. Just the chopper fuel needed to airlift the team close enough to sneak in to the final destination costs more than the scope does. Let's peg the scope at $1200 just for the sake of argument. (The government buys some optics that cost $12,000, just in case you were wondering.) You're looking at a $200 scope to park on your rifle, to go about learning the business of shooting.

Let us set aside for the moment the idea that a $200 scope and $1,000 worth of ammo will do a lot for your skills, a lot more than a $1,200 scope and no ammo. Let's say you buy the scope, put it on your rifle, and try it. You determine in short order that it just doesn't work for you, and sell it on the used market. Get $1,000 for it? Maybe. $900? More likely. You've already just lost more than the cheap scope would have cost to buy. And so we encounter yet again Sweeney's "Good enough" law. Gear that is good enough to improve your skills is plenty good enough to improve your skills. Will better gear make you learn faster? Maybe. Will it cost more? Certainly.

Now, this law runs counter to the advice given parents of aspiring musicians: buy the best instrument your budget can stand, because your child will make better music with it. The better the music, the higher the likelihood of their continuing. First of all, we aren't kids. (Well, some of us have grown up more than others, anyway.) Second, if you are hard enough on your gear that you break the inexpensive stuff, you are learning that you have to be more careful, at a lower cost than the mondo-expensivo gear. Failing to properly clean a $150 barrel that has to be replaced (something that can be done in half an hour, once the package from Brownells arrives) is a painful but forgivable lesson. To abuse a cut-rifling match barrel, fitted by someone such as White Oak, borders on the criminal. Not only will the tube alone cost you a house payment, but the time spent waiting for it to get turned and fitted will be in-

Do not worry about wearing out a rifle by practicing with it. There are plenty out there.

terminable or at least seem like it, as you berate yourself for such abuse.

So, buy what you like, buy what you can afford, and learn to use it. "But I want to buy what's best, and only buy once. I don't want to go through the 2-3-4 rifle dance that I've seen so many do." Too bad. The dance is informative. There is some information that you can only gain by doing it. Your buddy may laud bullpups, but only after you shoot one will you know if it works for you. He may say that the muzzle brake of his design tames the recoil of the latest long-range round. But only after you shoot it will you be able to tell if it is tamed enough for you.

Some things you've just got to go out and do for yourself. Which leads us to….

## Training

Just above, I mentioned trading shots at 1,000 yards. No, an SBR in 5.56 is not a particularly good tool for that task. However, there are people with whom you would be at a serious disadvantage, even if they were armed with that SBR and you had something more appropriate. They are called "skilled" and even "trained"

in the use of a rifle. Training matters. Some matters more than other training does, and this is again part of what you have to consider when selecting a school, class and instructor.

Again, what do you want to do? Now, for most tactical rifles, and tactical shooting, the maximum range you can expect most shots (and notice the use of "most" and "maximum") will be 300 yards. Yards, meters, whatever. However, the vast majority of the defensive shots you'll ever have to take (and this is a big assumption, that there will be any defensive shots you'll have to take) will be inside of 100 yards. And most of those, inside 50. And most of those, inside 25 yards.

Why will the majority of your shots be inside of 25 yards, "conversational distance?" Simple, outside of a military context, where you have rigid rules of engagements (and conversely, wide latitude within those rigid limits) you have to talk to someone in order to determine that they are in need of shooting – in fact, in need of shooting right now. A military unit, watching a group approach, will do a quick assessment: How are they dressed? What weapons are they carrying? Do any of them (as far as anyone can tell) look like

Technique is good. Knowing how to shoot around corners is good, but knowing not to stick around behind a car is even better.

known bad guys for the area? And, more importantly, a quick check with higher authority to make sure there aren't any friendly units operating in your area, friendlies who may be dressed like the local bad guys. Once all those questions have been answered in the column headed "Shoot Them, Shoot Them Now" and they are in a suitable location, you shoot them.

It may seem like that is the way big city police departments work, but it is far from it. And you, the non-sworn (we're all civilians; police and taxpayers alike) have even more restrictions on the use of lethal force. So it would serve you well to receive instruction in the use of your rifle, so you are familiar with it and don't have to distract your decision-making cycle of "Is this guy a threat, a threat enough that I have to shoot him?" with "where is the safety on this thing?"

You've no doubt seen or heard the commercial "parts is parts," right? Perhaps not. The point the company was trying to make was that not all parts were the same. And so, not all training is the same. Not just the qualitative differences, but the focus. I teach a patrol

rifle class, and the focus of the class (actually, several classes) is finely-tuned; it is to get police officers, who have had the basic handgun training their state and their department requires, tuned up on using a patrol rifle. Not competition, not long-range target shooting, and not small unit tactics facing potential belt-fed machineguns from another small unit. (At least I hope so. The day police officers have to worry about belt-feds and small unit tactics in the projects, we have a real problem.)

So, what do you want? Do you want to learn the basics? Search out the basics. You want to learn about team tactics? Then search that out. You'll have to do a bit of digging, as each instructor or school wants to get people in for instruction, but once you get past the "We're the best/oldest/most capable" advertising, the school info will tell you what they teach.

Attending a training academy is a multi-thousand dollar investment, so it bears some homework. Read their web pages. Write them emails asking about your desires, concerns and experience. Even ask around your

If you're going to work with people, you have to train with people. Ask what the class will be, and how it is done. It is your money and your safety on the line.

gun club. When I was running our club, it was a rare person (until we mounted an expedition to go to Gunsite) who had been to a shooting school of any kind. Nowadays, it would be a rare gun club that has no one who's been to a school of one kind or another.

Now, you have to have a big grain of salt with you when you talk to people about the shooting school they went to. We all know people who know more than anyone. We also know people who are not satisfied with anything. So if the club member you are talking to fits either of these (and these are just two prisms of experience learned) then keep that in mind. If so, of course they won't like anything they did.

If you aren't careful, you can become a training junkie. There are people who have gone to every school out there, who travel to two or three of them a year. Unless they took careful notes, and wrote themselves after-action reports, they won't be able to keep track of which was which, except for the last couple of classes they went to.

What should you look for in a training school and learning experience?

First, are the students happy? Yes, training academies are fun, and most people would be happy if you just lined them up and let them blast their ammo into the backstop non-stop. But sniff around the various forums and see if there are ongoing controversies with a particular school.

Second, what facilities do they have? A high-volume fun-and-gun class, held on a range with strict rules on shooting lines and "one-shot-a-second" firing restrictions is not a good pairing.

Where do they teach? Does it have a classroom, plumbing, food?

Another consideration: onsite medical expertise. Let's be up-front about this – firearms hurt. That's their whole purpose. If someone in the class goofs, and someone else takes a round, does the instructor have medical training? Is there a full-blown trauma kit onrange? Does someone there know how to use it?

Fourth, who is teaching? What experience do they have, both in shooting and in teaching. There are going to be a whole lot of veterans, returning from the Sandbox and the Mountain Resort with lots of trigger time. That does not mean they know how to teach. Many know only the military method of teaching, which really is not much fun when you're taking time off of work, and spending your own money to be instructed. Those who are smart will adjust.

And before you turn your nose up at the competition shooters who are "not tactical," let me give you a bit of inside info: the tactical shooters you may be seeking instruction from received a lot of training from the competitors. I've been seeing this of late, where a retired military instructor teaches me something "they developed in Delta/SEALS/SF" and when I see it I recognize it as something developed by USPSA/IPSC Grandmasters twenty years ago. The GMs went and taught the military, and it has been in the military so long that the guys and gals in uniform have forgotten where it came from.

The last teaching experience you can undergo is competition. Yes, yes, the gun shop commandos will declaim that it teaches the wrong lessons, and that you would be better off going through their training. Competition is as tactical as you make it. You can approach every stage with a completely tactical mindset. It won't win the match, but it builds good skills. Learning to shoot fast an accurately, while the clock is ticking, is a valuable skill. Every time you draw, move, reload and scan against the clock, you are building skills. I'm sure you've all hear the scale of competence. No? Here it is;

*Unconscious incompetence:* You don't know that you don't know.
*Conscious incompetence:* You know that you don't know.
*Conscious competence:* You know it, but you have to think about it, or you'll get it wrong.
*Unconscious competence:* You know it, and you don't have to think about it to do it right.

The more skills you can drill into your mind at the unconscious competence level, the less you'll have to think about when it is all on the line. Tell the gun shop commandos to buzz off, and get out and learn to handle your rifle like a pro.

Learn wherever you can learn, from whom you can learn, and process it all for your own use.

I hate to be so long on this, but training matters, and like buying gear there is no fast and easy, one-step method. You will have to do it over time. If you took one class, years ago, you are not nearly as good as you think. Your skills have faded, your reflexes dulled. If you never shoot in matches, because they are "not tactical" and "IPSC will get you killed" then you have passed up an opportunity to build unconscious competence in gunhandling.

**CHAPTER 2**

# Overview of Types

The rifle is an outgrowth of the musket, which was the basic infantry arms for centuries. We think of the musket exemplar as the Brown Bess, the British land Pattern Musket that began in the earliest years of the 18th century, and lasted to the middle of the 19th. But a smooth-bore shoulder arm was the basic tool of infantry from the middle of the 15th century onwards.

What the rifle did was increase potential accuracy, range, and power.

I say potential accuracy. Consider the Battle of Bunker Hill. The British march up, the finest professional army of the world at that moment in time. No one can stand before them and prevail. No one can stand up to them, period. A bunch of volunteers are on top of the hill, and the British march up to drive them off. In pretty much any other place and time, the result would be the same: the British would march, stop at a very short distance, level their arms, fire a volley, then charge with bayonets and drive the remaining opponents off the hill. The carnage would be impressive, and everyone would have learned their lesson.

Instead, the 3,000 British troops, after two assaults, take the hill only because the defenders have run out of ammo. They suffer 800 casualties, including 226 killed, and the percentage of those killed and wounded who happen to be officers are out of proportion to British combat experience. Why? The 2400 American defenders were not using issued muskets, firing in a volley on command, and trying to do so in a manner required by regulation. They were aiming.

The Americans suffered 305 wounded, 115 killed, and were not driven off and bayoneted as they fled, as the British might have expected. In fact, the "untrained" colonials conducted a fighting withdrawal that was so effective that they were even able to retrieve most of their wounded.

While the guns used technically weren't rifles, they *were* being used tactically. During the entire war, the British were most outraged that the colonials would actually aim – and not just aim at the troops, but at officers and non-commissioned officers. That just wasn't sporting.

Moreover, the problem with rifles then, and for a long time, was their slow rate of fire. And their lack of bayonets. A trained force of men, using muskets, could load and fire two shots a minute. A rifle, which required a patched ball, was more like a shot a minute. And if the force with muskets got close enough to charge, the lack of bayonets was most troublesome to the riflemen.

Fast-forward past the invention and adoption of the percussion cap to the invention of the Minie ball. Before retiring as a Colonel in the French Army, Claude-Etienne Minié (actually pronounced *meen-yay)* perfected the bullet which was to become named after him. The minie ball (the accent and capital "M" were dropped pretty quickly) is a cylindrical bullet with a point and a hollow base. The bullet is enough undersized that it will slide down the bore. When the powder burns, the pressure generated expands the base of the bullet, which grips the rifling, and thus spins the bullet.

A spinning object maintains stability around its center of gravity. A non-spinning one is more affected by air, a fact the knuckleball pitcher knows and uses to his advantage.

The minie ball thus allowed the user to load as fast as a smoothbore musket, but shoot with the accuracy of a rifle. That was what much of the American Civil War was fought with. Now, the actual effectiveness of the rifled musket in the Civil War is debated to this day. I've read analyses that decrease and increase claims of its effectiveness. I can't say.

Rifle types matter, and what you want them to do will determine how effective your tool is. DoD photo by Petty Officer 2nd Class Walter J. Pels, U.S. Navy.

Cartridges made rifles work better and faster and load more quickly, but black powder hindered that. Once we entered the era of magazine-fed, smokeless powder rifles, the stage was set for the tactical rifle. Too bad tactics had to catch up.

The armies of the world fought WWI with 20th-century rifles and 19th-century tactics. They fought WWII with 20th-century tactics, and many were still using 19th century rifles.

It wasn't until after WWII that rifles moved into the tactical era completely, and that brings us to the present day.

OK, tactical rifles can be broken down into a bunch of different types, but I'll take a straightforward mechanical approach. You've got your big-bores and small-bores, big in this context being .308, and small being everything under that. Yes, yes, yes, the AK fans will protest that the 7.62X39 is a big bore; it is after all the same bullet diameter as a 7.62 NATO/.308. However, where the AK spits a 123-grain bullet at something like 2250 or so (the nominal specs are higher, but the Soviets were not all that interested in making the nominal specs) the NATO load is a 147-grain bullet at 2700 fps. Now, if you shorten barrels you decrease those, but both suffer. It isn't like there is some magic to the AK bullet, where shortening the barrel doesn't harm the velocity.

So, we have the small ones: 5.45, 5.56, 6.5, 6.8 and 7.62X39. There are real and significant differences between those cartridges, but the rifles they are in are all essentially the same size, and in many instances identical rifles, with different bores, chambers and magazines. I mean, really, what is the difference in handling between an AK in 5.45, 5.56 or 7.62X39? None.

Perusing lists, it is easy to pick out the small ones. Their caliber gives them away.

The big bores are bigger rifles, simply to handle the physically larger cartridge, and to stand the mechanical forces of the heavier bullet at high velocity. Here, age is the detail that will likely sort them out. A self-loading rifle that hails from before 1970 or so is likely to be a big-bore. There are exceptions, of course. The Galil, for one, is made (or was made) in both 5.56 and 7.62 NATO. However, while the 5.56 Galil is more common, especially in the form of the Century Arms Golani Sporter, the 7.62 is a definite collector's beast, beast both in weight and cost. So: early rifle, probably a big bore. Later one, probably a small one.

Second, we have the direct-gas guns (mostly the AR) and the various piston systems. The piston systems can be long-stroke like the AK, SIG 556, Galil, and Garand and the short-stroke like the M1 Carbine, FAL, and M1A/M14. There are others; the CETME/G3, for example, uses a roller-locked delayed blowback. The French FAMAS uses a lever-cammed delayed blowback. You won't see many of those; they were only imported in small numbers in the semi-auto form (I don't know if the select-fire version made it here or not, some must have) but at the last price I recall, $8,000 for a semi-auto rifle is a bit steep.

The form of the gas system matters primarily in how many parts will there be to keep track of in disassembly and cleaning. If it was made for military use, then it is probably pretty durable, reliable, and easy to get apart and clean. Still, fewer parts means less to track and clean.

The last category is the bullpup, which can be any of the above.

Just so we're clear, and there are no misunderstandings or hard feelings, I want to explain my position on bullpup rifles, designs and use: I really don't care. I don't care that a bunch of people think they are the greatest thing not just since sliced bread, but since the bread slicer, even. I don't care that they've been working at it for nearly a century, that many countries have adopted bullpup designs (and many also dropped them) and that the advantages are obvious. I just don't find them to be better than non-bullpups.

Now, before we go all quasi-religious and discuss the attributes of bullpups vis-à-vis regular rifles, let's be clear about just what a bullpup rifle is. Conjure up in your mind an image of a regular rifle. (Or just look at one of the photos in another chapter.) From the part against your shoulder forward, we have buttplate, stock, action/receiver (complete with magazine or magazine well) chamber, barrel and muzzle.

A bullpup rifle takes the essentially unused portion, the buttstock, and pushes the action/receiver and all else forward of it, back to the buttplate. In so doing, the bullpup rifle is made shorter by the collapsed distance, and thus more compact.

The big advantage is the shortness. A rifle that has everything else the same (just for the purposes of a mental exercise in 3-D modeling) will be shorter by the distance collapsed. So if we, for example, were to take a classic battle rifle of the middle of the previous century, like the M-14, at its usual length of 44 inches, and collapse the receiver back to the buttplate, a distance of a foot, we end up with a theoretical, 3-D mentally-modeled M-14 bullpup with a length of 32 inches. If, in the design we dispense with the overly long flash hider, and trim the barrel (nominally 22 inches) to a useful 18 inches, we can theoretically come up with a .308 thumper that is only 27 to 28 inches long.

In mechanized travel (helicopters, armored vehicles, up-armored Humvees or SUVs) compact is king. Trying to unfold oneself from a vehicle with a 44-inch-long weapon is difficult at best. The compactness of the bullpup is thus very alluring. And not new, either. There was an experimental bullpup bolt-action rifle, the Thornycroft carbine, in 1901. The French (the French?) experimented with a self-loading bullpup rifle in WWI. But the massive increase in troops riding in vehicles in WWII lead to the interest in bullpup designs in the post-war period.

The advantage of the bullpup is also gained without a loss in effectiveness. A USGI M4 is 33 inches long with the stock extended, and 30 inches with it collapsed. However, the barrel is only 14.5 inches long, and to make the rifle any more compact, you need to trim the barrel. A Colt Commando, with an 11.5-inch barrel, is a lot more compact (it has, after all, had three full inches trimmed off of it) but the gain in compactness is bought at the cost of lost muzzle velocity. A bullpup gains you compactness without the loss of muzzle velocity, as you need not trim the barrel to make it short.

And that about sums up the advantages of a bullpup: compactness. The drawbacks? Plenty.

First up, moving the muzzle back a foot makes it that much closer to your head/ears and forward hand. Muzzle blast will thus be greater for any given caliber

or load. Now, since we all shoot with earmuffs (or "defenders" as the British call them) muzzle blast doesn't matter much. But, if you ever needed to shoot without hearing protection, your ears are going to get hammered more than they otherwise would. Also, putting a muzzle brake on a bullpup creates an "interesting" firearm. Interesting in that if the muzzle brake/compensator is at all effective, the hairs on the backs of your arms are going to be seared off.

The most effective/ferocious muzzle brake I've ever shot is the McArthur PGRS brake. It is large, seriously engineered and vented, and it is a flamethrower of a brake. I've seen them in use, stripping paint off of an adjacent wall. I once fired a 11.5-inch-barreled M16 that had a PGRS installed. I was lucky to escape with any forearm hair left, and I thought for a few shots that my earmuffs were going to get blasted off. I shud-

In the wide open spaces, something with reach is what you need. And as the British learned on Bunker and Breed's hills, aimed fire does more than just blasting. DoD photo by Sean McKenna, U.S. Army.

der to think what it would be like, using a PGRS on a bullpup.

The really big deals on bullpup drawbacks are the matters of trigger design, manual of arms, and empty ejection. And a final problem is safety in the case of a ballistic disassembly.

Trigger design is simple – you can move the receiver back into the buttstock, but you have to leave the trigger and pistol grip right where they were. Unless someone wants to try and market a design with a left-hand trigger, back at the buttplate, for a right-handed (and right-shouldered) rifle, the trigger stays where it was. This means that the pistol grip and trigger, which used to be at the rear of the action/receiver on the regular rifle, are now out in front of those parts on the bullpup.

The trigger needs some sort of linkage to get the trigger action back to the receiver, where it can activate the firing mechanism, which is usually a hammer. As a result, bullpups tend to have trigger pulls that range from "spongy and vague" to "this thing sucks" in their triggers. Now, to the "modern" designer, who view those using weapons as ones who don't really aim and shoot, they just hose an area with full-auto fire or bursts until the air-delivered ordnance arrives, a crisp trigger is over-rated. Those of us who can actually shoot feel otherwise. As a result, many designers and adherents really don't "get" the complaint by users that the bullpup of their dreams just can't be shot accurately or effectively.

The manual of arms thing is simple: having spent decades learning to stuff a magazine into the rifle "out front" we now have to figure a new way, one where the magazine well is nearly in our armpits. The usual speed-reload, of hit the mag button with the firing hand while the old magazine drops free, and meanwhile grab a fresh one and stuff it in as the old one falls away, doesn't work. For one thing, the mag button isn't near our firing hand. The magazine is some six inches or more away from the pistol grip. And in many bullpups, the magazine doesn't fall free. Finally, stuffing the new one in place is more difficult, because, as I said, the mag well is nearly in our armpit, and leaving the rifle mounted ends up being a contortionist/chiropractic/yoga exercise.

There is also the matter of safety buttons and charging handles. If the design is a modification, then the charging handle, designed and located for use in one location, is now someplace else. And the safety button either has to have linkages to connect it to the firing

Ever wonder why the military doesn't get all warm and fuzzy over handguns? Consider this Marine, with a dozen HE grenades for his M203. DoD photo by Cpl. Daniel M. Moman, U.S. Marine Corps.

mechanism, or it simply blocks the trigger (a bad idea in many instances).

Finally, there's the matter of ejection of empties. If the action/receiver is at the buttplate, that means it is directly under your face. So, if you try to switch shoulders to shoot, the ejection port is where your face will rest, and any attempt to shoot means a hot case whipping out at impressive speeds, directly into your cheekbone. Ouch. Now, bullpups designed from the ground up solve that by various means. But bullpup-mods, existing rifles or designs stuffed into bullpup stocks, really can only be shot right-handed.

Ground-up bullpup designs solve the problem by means of two approaches: they either arranged the empties to be dropped straight down out of the receiver, such as the FNH-USA PS-90, or they have some sort of empty case handling gear, as in the FNH-USA FS-2000 or the Kel-Tec FSB, where the empties are pulled out of the chamber, then handed off to the ejection tube, which allows them to simply be shoved forward, one at a time, until they fall out the front of the tube.

The last part brings us also to the safety issue. In the case of a blown case, a plugged bore, or some other problem that leads to a blown rifle, modern designs protect the shooter. I've seen ARs turned into shrapnel that did not harm the shooter. Not all rifles will be safe in all instances, but a bullpup is particularly troublesome. Since your face is directly under the receiver, it is difficult to protect the shooter from a blown gun, without making the thing a pound or two heavier. The firearms equivalent of a drag-racing transmission blanket (a Kevlar cover to contain blown transmission parts) has not yet been invented. So, bullpup designs will add extra steel, in a plate between the shooters face and the receiver.

Lastly, and this is an entirely subjective impression, bullpups just don't handle right. Now, it may be akin to a life-long rear wheel car owner getting into his first front wheel drive car and complaining "this thing doesn't handle right" but I've handled a lot of guns, and shot a lot of different ones, in decades of shooting. And for me, bullpups just don't work. First, the handling is neutral or even butt-heavy. Granted, I learned to shoot rifles first on a Lee-Enfield MkIII* and then an M1 Garand, both definitely nose-heavy thumpers. But I like a bit of weight out front on something as light as an AR, too.

Perhaps this is akin to shotgun shooters; skeet and trap shooters, as well as duck and goose hunters, like weight out front to keep the swing going. Hunters who go after quail and other fast, close, direction-changing birds, like weight more in the middle, so they can keep up with the smaller, faster targets.

What it comes down to is simply this: does it work for you?

A comparison would be the QWERTY keyboard, vs. the Dvorak keyboard. The QWERTY (so-named after the first six keys on the upper left row) was designed almost a century and a half ago. Ostensibly to avoid the interlocking of keys (typewriters for nearly a century actually caused little arms, each with a letter on the end, to swing up and smack a ribbon and transferred a letter-shaped ink blot onto the paper in the machine) the design was not laid out for the most-efficient need for the letters themselves. That was the Dvorak keyboard. Every decade or so since being patented in 1936, the Dvorak will rise to interest, as its advocates tell of the virtues of faster typing, less work and strain, etc. And most of us who type look at it, go "meh" and keep what we have, which is the good ol' QWERTY.

The last half-century have given us a steady supply of bullpups. The earliest post-war was the Enfield EM-2, a collaboration between the British and the Belgians in 7X43, meant to replace the .303 Lee-Enfield. Despite trying again and again, the British could not get the obstinate American Army ordnance experts to see the utility of a medium-bore round, as well as the bullpup, and with the decision to go with the (what would soon be) 7.62X51 NATO round, the bullpup design was dropped too.

In 1977, Steyr unveiled the game-changer: the AUG. The AUG Universal Army Rifle offered more than just a bullpup design: it was made in large part from high-tech plastics, polymers. The barrel could be changed in seconds, without tools. The bolt could be re-assembled by the user to offer left-handed ejection. And, to make things fully complicated, the trigger was different: there was no selector. If you wanted semi-auto fire, you simply pressed the trigger back. To get full-auto fire, you clutched the trigger back. Now, my father is no weapons designer. He does, however, have a take on design that perhaps exceeds that of the AUG designers: he was the beneficiary of Uncle Sam's Walking Tour of Northern France and Germany, 1944-45. When I told him of the design, his first comment was "And how much ammo will the new guys burn up, in full-auto fire, under stress, before they learn to control it?"

Apparently it's not a problem to the militaries of the world, as it has been adopted by some two dozen countries. (But I'd very curious as to how the peacetime-trained armies of Europe, using the AUG, fared when they first got into a shooting engagement with them)

Right on its heels in 1978 was the French FAMAS, which is not polymer, and has some interesting and perhaps not so pleasant aspects as well. The FAMAS mechanism is not a locked one, like those of the AR, AUG, and many others. What it is, is a lever-delayed blowback. When the rifle is fired, the pressurized case pushes back on the bolt. The bolt, with a lever inside, has to cam an additional weight back, prior to unlatching from the receiver. When I finally managed to see the schematics, and watch an animation of the system, I have to say I was unimpressed. My initial thought was "How do they keep from busting cases? Well, apparently the answer was simple: they made their own ammo, ammo stout enough for the task. They loaded steel-cased ammo. When the French decided to not make their own ammo but buy NATO-spec ammo from others, they began to have problems. (Proving once again that the selective parsimony of elected officials is never to be discounted as a non-problematic variable.) Being the French, I imagine they'll complain bitterly about the ammo others make, while quietly trying to adjust the FAMASs to use the "foreign" ammo. And, the engineering changes to "adapt" the FAMAS will probably be greater than the savings of buying "less expensive" NATO-spec ammo.

The British dove back into the bullpup fray with the SA80, which actually began production in 1985. As a bullpup design it has all the drawbacks, combined with several other problems: as a rifle it can barely be called reliable, and to use the word "durable" in describing it would be hype on the level of P.T. Barnum. In fact, it proved so bad (some parts simply broke in handling, others could be busted in being pressed against the soldiers' gear, while being carried) that the Ministry of Defence turned the whole lot of them over to H-K (then a subsidiary of British Aerospace) for re-design and rebuild.

Despite that, any chance they get, British Special Forces use the oft-maligned M16/M4 instead of the SA80, known in the British Army as the L85A1 IW.

The Chinese (the mainland Commies, not the Taiwanese good guys) are looking at an adapted bullpup AK in a new cartridge. Of all the basic mechanisms to adapt to the bullpup format, I would pick the AK last.

To add to the mystery, the Chinese have adopted a new cartridge that seems to defy the basics of known ballistic art: it shoots more accurately than any AK made, and the bullet produces more penetration of barriers than any other bullet of its size. Two ideas come to mind: that some Chinese commissar stuck his neck out, and until he's promoted high enough that the whole thing an be covered up and forgotten, it will be hyped. Or it is a deliberate false lead, meant to distract Western small arms designers. We'll see.

And so it is with bullpups. The adherents beat the drum, some like it, some don't, some try it and some don't, some buy them and most don't, and it goes quiet again for a few years or a decade.

But that doesn't keep me from trying them again, and telling you what I've found.

One more type is the bolt action. While the bolt action design was perfected (in the minds of many) in 1898 by Peter Paul Mauser, it had its heyday as a battle rifle in WWI. By WWII, it was clearly not the weapon of choice, but the institutional inertia of various Armies around the world, and the lack of willingness to test and debug/adopt new rifles, kept a lot of the combatants in WWII using bolt action rifles. They still have many adherents. I can appreciate the durability of a Moisin-Nagant rifle, I just don't want to be stuck with one if there are better choices. Especially if I need to deal with more than I can handle with five relatively slow bolt-action shots, and be left with a five-foot pig-sticker once it is empty.

So for us, in the tactical sense, a bolt-action rifle is a sniper rifle. If it is not mechanically capable of sub-MOA, forget it. And if the total package has some drawback (like a sucky trigger, shoddy ammo or a crappy scope) that precludes shooting sub-MOA, then it gets left off the list, too.

Now, in an emergency, there are a lot of rifles that would serve quite well. Yes, emergencies do that. Were I stuck in a backwater BFE where there was no other choice, you bet I'd find a way to get the Yugo I just found started, running, and filled with anything that would burn as fuel. But, that is an emergency. If I'm headed out on an expedition, I'd sure as heck insist on something besides a Yugo with bald tires and a loud engine knock.

And so it is with rifles: in an emergency you may have to use whatever you can find, scrounge or assemble from parts. But starting out, you want good gear. So get it.

**CHAPTER 3**

# The AK

The Kalashnikov is a brutally simple, almost crude design, meant to be issued to a mob of semi-literate conscripts, and intended to out-survive its users. That it can be "cleaned" by taking the top cover off (or not) and swishing it around in a reasonably clean puddle is a feature some find endearing. And some find aggravating.

You see, the simplicity of the AK is gained at the cost of ergonomics and accuracy. Oh, you can occasionally find an AK that will shoot under 3 MOA (roughly three inches at 100 yards) with match ammo, but most are only a bit better than "minute of person" at 100 yards.

And unless you re-build (or build from scratch) an AK with actual human engineering in it, none will be much more than passably ergonomic.

Now, some view the whole attention to ergonomics as an affectation. "It's an AK, it is supposed to be crude" is the usual comeback. Well, pardon me if I want something that is more ergonomic than a rock, thank you very much, comrade.

The big advantage of the AK is its very lack of expense, at least while the imports are still flowing. When the suits figure out a way to strangle the flow, the prices will go up, and when they go up, buyers will expect features. Some already expect features, and for that we can be thankful for the market system, the worst economic system ever – except for all the rest (to paraphrase Winston Churchill).

A crude but reliable rifle that costs $450, is something that will sell. If the price doubles, guys are going to expect a bit of refinement, maybe more than just a little bit at that. So, we'll look at a very basic AK, one that has been built to be done right, and then one that has been overhauled and has refinements, accessories and performance as well.

A policeman in the Afghan Border Police gets marksmanship instruction from Sgt. Webb. DoD photo by Tech. Sgt. Francisco V. Govea II, U.S. Air Force.

The Century AK is built on a US-made milled receiver.

For those asleep in a cave for decades, the AK is a long-stroke piston design, with the gas system on top of the barrel, a 30-round magazine underneath, and a pistol grip behind, with a stock on the back end. The receivers of AKs have been made with machined forgings, billets, and stamped. (I don't recall ever seeing or hearing of, a polymer-based AK, but I'd bet someone is working on it.)

AKs, or AK derivatives, have been made in 5.56/.223, 5.45 Soviet, 7.62X39, 8mm Mauser and .308. I've heard of a serious experimenter who tried to build an AK in 6.8 Remington SPC, but the technical difficulties just kept piling up. Once he realized that there was no way to fit any kind of a reliable or high-capacity magazine to the gun, he gave up on it. I'd bet, with a full CAD/CAM setup, and a manufacturer to make what was needed, it could be done. But to what end? The 6.8 is a round that users expect to deliver MOA, and out of an AK it would simply disappoint. Best not to even start going there.

The AK has several strengths. Chiefly, it is uncommonly inexpensive to manufacture. I'd guess, if you wanted to set up a modern, efficient manufactur-ing plant, that you could produce AKs (leaving aside the extra costs of union labor) for about $200 each. "What? Two hundred bucks? Then why does any AK, even an imported one, cost over four hundred?" Simple: volume. The local manufacturers don't have enough volume to bring down costs, and the importers aren't about to price them a nickel less than what they can get. It's that market economy thing, again. Unless you're sure to get the volume of sales, who wants to invest in the stamping machinery, the machining and the investment casting, to bring the cost down to almost nothing? And if you're exporting, you know the crazy Americans will spend $400-450 on an AK, so why discount it to the importer in the US?

The AK is durable, although it is not impervious to abuse. It is reliable, although it is not the implacable engine of destruction that some (on both sides) seem to think. And it is easy to use. The controls are large and easy to explain.

On the downside, we have the appalling lack of accuracy. American shooters, accustomed to at least the level of accuracy demonstrated by hunting rifles, where a lever-action .30-30 will do 2-3 MOA, are sometimes surprised and always unamused by an AK delivering 5+ MOA. Given one with a few rounds through it, a lack of care, and some crappy surplus ammo, brought over in the bilge of a freighter 20 years ago, and you might be good to be getting 8 MOA. I have been amused on several occasions, to watch someone bench-rest an AK, expecting to get significantly better accuracy than they just go shooting it offhand. Their disappointment is universal.

Now, that isn't because the system can't do it. My friend David Fortier has visited Finland several times, and on one occasion he was merrily plinking down reactive targets at 450 meters with an AK. However, it was a Finnish-made AK. A forged receiver with a match barrel screwed into it, and Lapua ammo. That does not describe the combination most-often seen here stateside.

Ammo isn't ammo, when it comes to the AK. Some 25 years ago, the VP of my gun club and I went in on a bulk purchase of ammo for our M1A rifles. This was, as best I recall, surplus British ammo, most likely Radway Green. RG was one of the remaining ordnance factories left after the British decided that owning most of the world was not a good investment strategy and pulled back to just the British Isles. Since they no longer needed (or had) a world-ranging army, they didn't need more than one ordnance factory. RG was it. (I mean, how much ammo do you need for an army not even as big as the USMC, and with not much political taste for exercising it?)

RG made ammo for the L1A1 rifle, the license-built FAL the British Army used until the spectacularly crappy SA80 replaced it. This ammo was cheap, even by the costs of the halcyon days of cheap surplus ammo. The reason? It was crusty green from corrosion. Neither we nor our rifles cared, as it shot just fine. I joked at the time that our ammo had probably ridden in the bilge of a cargo ship, down

> **THIS AMMO WAS CHEAP, EVEN BY THE COSTS OF THE HALCYON DAYS OF CHEAP SURPLUS AMMO. THE REASON? IT WAS CRUSTY GREEN FROM CORROSION.**

The Centurion has a railed polymer handguard, a place to mount lights.

The stock and pistol grip are also synthetic, but feel free to swap them out for wood for a period-correct build.

to the Falklands and back. Then it was sold to the crazy yanks for the simple reason that we'd buy it.

AK ammo is all over the map. You can find stuff that was carefully crafted, meant to be used "by *Spetnaz* snipers in the Afghan campaign" and you can find stuff that appears to be reloaded in Pakistan by small shopkeepers near the border, using a ball peen hammer, a rusty nail and pliers.

The AK, even on well-made samples, is a mass of edges, sharp parts, sheet metal stampings and protrusions. A well-made one will have the edges "broken" or knocked off, but they still protrude. The safety is the ejection port cover, and you cannot push the safety off without taking one of your hands off the rifle. The magazines, while durable, are heavy, and also require two-handed manipulation.

The stock, as designed, is too short for most normal Americans, being designed with winter-dressed diminutive Soviet troopers in mind. The forearm does not protect the hand from heat, and as the AK heats up it can become interesting as to just how you're going to hold on to it. And finally, the sights are old-school in the extreme. They are a post out front, and a notch rear that is at the front of the receiver. So, you have a sight system that while fast to use, is not all that precise, and

not conducive to anything more than combat-range hosing. Now, I've used an AK (an AK-74, to be precise) on the 300-meter computerized popups on a National Guard base, and shot a 20 out of 20 with it. But I really had to work on the shots past 200 meters. Shooting the course with an AR, and its aperture sight, a 20/20 is something I can practically do with my eyes closed.

So, what makes an AK so tactical? Go re-read the list of positives again. In most armed encounters, in most instances, people are shot within, or close to, conversational distances. Why? Again: In a whole lot of instances, you have to talk to someone before you can determine that you have to shoot them.

## Century International Arms

As importers and manufacturers go, Century is one of the biggies, if not the biggest. And even they had headaches to deal with. When they were importing AK kits, they found many out of spec. As a result, they had to either scrap guns, or make replacement parts. Then the big change in interpretation happened. The government, in its infinite wisdom (one of these days they are going to notice that I'm so snarky, and there will be headaches for me. Until then, too bad!) decided that barrels were not a normal wear item, and a replacement

The Krebs safety allows you to keep your hand on the pistol grip, and still work the safety.

The Krebs loading plate provides an indicating plate for your reloads.

The big problem with the AK is that no one has fingers long enough to reach the safety and still keep a firing grip on the pistol grip.

If you really need a scope on your AK, don't use the funky Soviet sidemount. Go and do it right with a Krebs.

part. Rational? No. We all know that barrels wear. But, as a scheme to make parts kits importation too expensive to be economically viable, it was a smart move and only a tiny bit fascistic.

Once the supply of imported kits that had Commie-made barrel dried up, the parts kits had to have new, American-made barrels. And that sowed the seed of the next step, which Century has taken.

Enter the all American-made AK! That's right, a rifle where all the parts are made here in the USA. No need to worry about 922(r) compliance, because that only applies to imported rifles.

The Centurion 39 rifle starts as an eleven-pound block of 4140 steel. It is them machined out on a numerical machining center, computer-controlled and identical to each other. Once the receiver is done, it

gets the other parts installed. The barrel has a Century-designed muzzle brake on it, their V-shaped Chevron brake, to dampen felt recoil. Now, the recoil of the 7.62X39 is not all that oppressive. And at a bit over eight pounds (hey, it is a milled receiver, remember?) the round is not going to push you around. But a brake is better than just a flash hider for a lot of people. If it offends your sensibilities, then you can just swap it out for the flash hider or slant brake of your heart's desire.

The safety, receiver cover and internal parts are all normal AK parts, and made here in the US. And that wasn't so hard, since a lot of the internals were already being made here. You see, the incremental steps by the anti-gunners to try and control the AK importation simply made it incrementally possible to begin parts production. The trigger mechanisms are already being

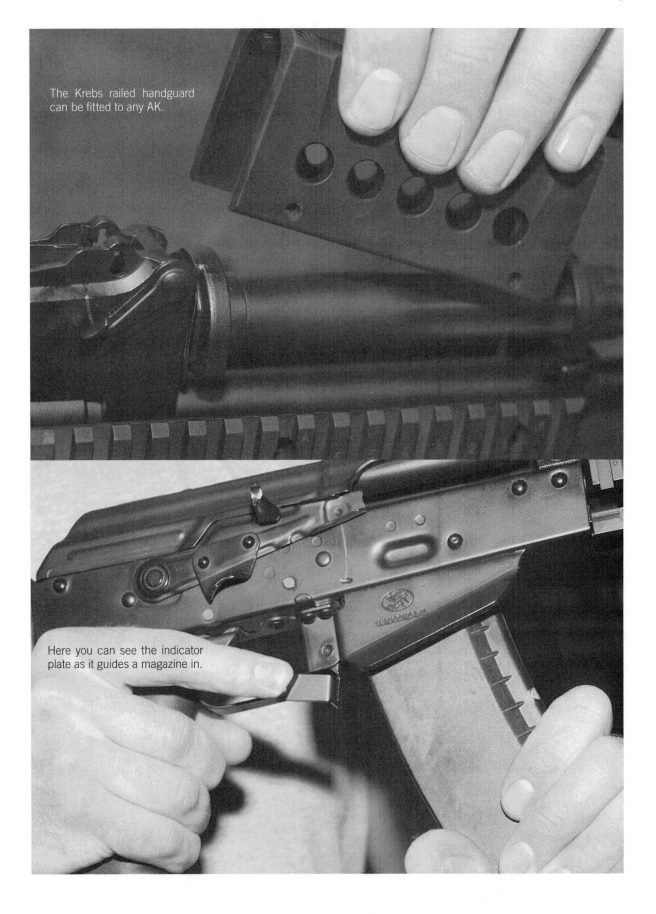

The Krebs railed handguard can be fitted to any AK.

Here you can see the indicator plate as it guides a magazine in.

Reliable? Come on, it's an AK.

made, and have been for a decade. Ditto the gas piston and the furniture.

The furniture is all synthetic, black, and the forearm upper and lower have rails included in the mold that makes them. So you get black synthetic furniture, rails ready to go, and all in an all-US made AK.

Looking at it, the only parts that really took some work were the bolt and carrier, gas tube and the front sight. Pretty much everything else was already being made, including the receivers.

The Centurion 39 is a solid and basic AK-47, and as such is amenable to any level of modification and dolling-up you'd care to subject it to. As long as you keep in mind that AK dimensions and specifications wander all over the place, you'll be able to fit just about anything you'd want to it to make it the AK you desire. Or, swap out the synthetic furniture and muzzle brake for wood and a slant brake, and have an AK that is a clone of a pre-1950 rifle.

Function? Let's not be silly here. It is an AK, which means it shot everything I had to feed it, shot to the sights, shot as well as you'd expect surplus ammo to shoot, and it never failed.

Cost? Here you're going to balk. At $800 or so, it is priced higher than that of the imports. However, if you are going to be serious about "Made in America" you owe yourself to take a look. And the price of the imports won't stay down forever. One day you'll wake up, and realize that there are no more "cheap Romy-made AKs" to be had, and if we haven't built up an American manufacturing base for AKs, then we're all out of everyone's favorite blaster.

## Krebs

Marc Krebs is a custom gun builder of many years standing. He was building IPSC Open pistols back when the Clintons were still aspiring to enter the front door of the White House. When AKs began to be imported, he saw the promise they held, and immediately began working on AKs. What he found was that while the Soviets were happy with an appalling lack of standardization and quality control, Marc wasn't. As he progressed through the building of rifles, he began to produce more and more of his own parts to replace the crappy, unheat-treated components and just plain bad ergonomics.

What he does now is take imported Arsenal rifles, and rebuilds them entirely. In order to bring them to the standard his customers require, he has to do some pretty impressive things. First of all, the rifles are imported without pistol grips. So he yanks out the trunnions, welds up the old rivet holes, re-drills rivet holes, and installs a proper pistol grip and trunnion for the stock of your choice. Since this brings it under the purview of importation and assault weapon regs, he has to make them 922(r) compliant. No problem, since he is tossing out the old trigger anyway. He installs new, American-made trigger parts, pistol grips, stocks, etc.

Since he's putting a new trunnion in, you can have the stock you want. Want a solid stock? No problem. Want a folder? No problem, either, which one do you want? You just have to insist on something that actually exists, or be willing to pay the R&D to come up with a new design.

But Marc doesn't stop there. While he offers regular models, you can have extra features (or not) as you wish. One I like is the loading platform. The AK magazine has to be inserted by hooking the front and then rocking it in at the rear. It is important to keep the magazine vertical to the axis of the rifle, or it won't work. The loading platform is a plate welded to the receiver on the right side, that provides a surface to index the magazine on. Slap the magazine against the plate, hook the front, rock it back, you're done. No worries about keeping things in line.

One aspect of the AK that really sucks is its safety. It is far enough from your shooting hand that you cannot reach it to push it on or off without taking your hand off the pistol grip. For the Soviets, this wasn't a problem. It may not have even risen to the level of notice. I mean, a few years before the AK was unveiled they commonly had assaulting infantry riding on top of racing armored vehicles. The idea of quick weapons manipulation for the individual was not just far from their minds – it wasn't even a concern. Today, we view such things differently. To make the AK safety more user-friendly, Krebs designed a replacement with a shelf in the middle, close enough that you can reach it. You still have to have a strong finger, but you can reach it.

> **THE IDEA OF QUICK WEAPONS MANIPULATION FOR THE INDIVIDUAL WAS NOT JUST FAR FROM THEIR MINDS – IT WASN'T EVEN A CONCERN.**

Rifles he has overhauled get Marc Kreb's seal.

Flash hider? Muzzle brake? The AK can do it.

And it fits all your other AKs, too, if you want to upgrade.

The AK, designed in the immediate post-war period, has no provision for mounting accessories of any kind. If you want, Krebs can put a scope mount on the side of the receiver, to accept a standard Soviet scope mount. While this is correct for a stock Soviet rifle, it sucks for anything else. Krebs makes a receiver rail that rides over the receiver cover and provides a place to mount a scope.

In the modern world, if you don't have a lot of rail estate on your rifle, it isn't really a "tactical" rifle. You've got to have enough rail space to mount 17 pounds worth of electronics, lights and accessories (I swear to god, one of these days we're going to see a Picatinny mount for an IPod, if it hasn't already happened) and the AK in its original form definitely misses out here. Well, not a Krebs. The Krebs AK forearm bolts on, is made of aluminum, and it has plenty of rail space.

On the muzzle, you can have a flash hider, a muzzle brake, a combo setup, whatever your heart's desire may be. Those of you lucky enough to live in a locale where they are allowed can even have it SBR'd and made compact and cute. I, alas, do not live in such a place, so I have to look on in envy.

Once you've gotten the full Krebs treatment, your AK is a far cry from what Mikhail Kalashnikov came up with. It is more ergonomic, it has greater options, and it works as well as any ever did, perhaps better than most.

Pfc. Bass and an Afghan national Policeman conduct a patrol in the village of Pir Zadeh. Notice that the policeman cannot reach his safety, with his hand on the pistol grip, which is common. DoD photo by Staff Sgt. Dayton Mitchell, U.S. Air Force.

# The M14/M1A

After WWII, the US Army was the big deal on the dry parts of the planet. The US Navy and the USMC held sway over the wet portions, and the Army Air Corps, soon to be the US Air Force, commanded the air. Yes, the armies of the Soviets were an awesome force, but they could not project their force beyond the European/Asian continents (admittedly, a large area) and if push came to shove, we had the atom bomb and they didn't. Which was a situation similar to what the British Army faced in the latter part of the 19th century: "Whatever else, we have the Maxim, and they do not" was the attitude the British carried with them when dealing with the locals. Of course, that didn't work out so well when they finally bumped up against the Boers, but that is for a different book. And the Soviets soon got The Bomb anyway.

Military theorists who were not wedded to fighting the previous war were looking toward post-atomic combat as the norm, even before the Russkies got nukes. And in that maelstrom, we wanted US soldiers, Marines and sailors to be not just dominant, but predominant. For that, they needed a better rifle than the one we had. All during WWII, the Garand had served us well, but to get more you have to have more. The biggest problems seen with the Garand centered around the feeding system; the en-bloc clips. If you loaded and then fired a few rounds, you couldn't "top off." You had to eject the rounds you had, and stuff a fresh eight-round clip in.

The dropped rounds were lost, down in the dust, mud or water. And soldiers desired more firepower, so a cross between the Garand and the BAR seemed like a good idea. Keep that "seemed" firmly in mind, now and in the future. An eight-shot full-auto rifle isn't much use. So, the Garand had to be boosted in capacity. A 20-shot en-bloc clip would be goofy. So, a box magazine it was. Now, you may ask, "Why not just build a Garand with a BAR magazine?" They did. But that wasn't good enough.

The Springfield Armory SOCOM II, the current top of the line M14 descendant, in an Vltor stock.

So, the government, via the US Army, spent the better part of a decade, and millions of dollars, to develop the M14. It improved on the gas system of the Garand, being a lot less sensitive and a lot more forgiving of powders and bullet weights ("sensitive" and "forgiving" being relative terms, of course). It used the same rotating bolt design as the Garand, improved with a roller bearing around the right-hand locking lug, to reduce frictional forces on the op rod cam surfaces. It had a flash hider, and the sights were as good as the Garand, basically being click-adjustable target sights.

Underneath, the magazine was a steel box, detachable, holding 20 rounds of the new .30 rifle cartridge, the 7.62X51 (in civvies, known as the .308 Winchester). It was a shorter .30-06 (basically, if not exactly) and took advantage of denser "ball" powders to deliver pretty much the same performance as the .30-06 in a shorter package.

The M14 was intended to replace not just the Garand, but everything in the inventory: BAR, M1 Garand, M1 Carbine, M3 sub-machinegun, and even in some minds the 1911A1 pistol. It failed, not just slightly, but spectacularly, in everything but replacing the Garand. How'd we get there? Why did it fail? What did we do about it? Why am I asking so many questions?

Here"'s why: right after WWII, there were a number of studies done, both here in the US and abroad, about just what had happened in the latest fracas. Basically, they all came to the same conclusion: shooting at enemy soldiers beyond 300 yards was not merely target shooting, but a waste of ammo. The experiences of the target-shooting community had misled everyone. Lying on one's stomach, on a freshly-mowed, flat target range, calmly gauging wind speed and distance, to plop a bullet through a six-foot square target frame at 1,000 yards was not the reality of combat. Instead, it was trying to tag a moving, partially-obscured enemy soldier across the street, a soldier who really didn't want to get shot, before he shot you. It was dealing with waves of Communist Chinese assaults, at night, on a frozen ridgeline in Korea.

Where I think things went wrong was in the extreme measures the anti-target range advocates proposed: high volumes of essentially unaimed fire, multi-

Topped with a Zeiss red-dot sight, the SOCOM II is plenty fast.

The little, bitty lug that is the cause of problems. The government couldn't be bothered to saw that off and thereby give us taxpayers some of our money back.

bullet loads, and more. Faced with the idea of trying to supply the troops with enough ammo to essentially "hose the countryside," the Army was not happy with the thoughts or suggestions of the researchers – especially when the "solution" to the problems volume fire brought with it was reduced caliber.

So, instead of taking a middle path between precision power and low-caliber hosing – an approach advocated by the British, among others – we stuck with what we had: a full-power .30 cartridge, with range and hitting power. Basically, it was a machinegun round stuffed into rifles. Instead of the .280 British round, which was a 7mm bullet of 139 grains at a nominal 2500 fps, the US Army insisted on a full-power cartridge: the .308-inch bullet of 150 grains at 2800 fps. (At this point, it is worth noting that the 6.8 RemSPC and the 6.5 Grendel bracket the original British specs; the 6.8 is a 110-grainer at 2600 fps, and the Grendel is a 129-grainer at 2550. Both have fierce advocates, and are seen as big steps up from the lowly 5.56 we now use.)

Oh, and "nominal?" A very useful word, which means the accepted, defined or average size/weight/income of a person, object or process. So, the nominal velocity of 2500 fps means that that was the figure the rifle designers and ammo makers strive for, but not necessarily the exact figure achieved by each and every production lot of ammo.

But what about the rifles? The .280 had been intended to be used first in a bullpup rifle, one of the great design attractants to inventers. As I've said, bullpup advocates are kind of like the non-QWERTY keyboard advocates, those who advocate the Dvorak keyboard, who will countenance no compromise or any criticism of their champion. Resistance to the bullpup design has been even stronger than that of smaller cartridges, and thus they have rarely caught on.

Faced with resounding uninterest in the bullpup, FN desired to have their original FAL design accepted in a smaller cartridge, the 7.92X33. (Yes, the German Stg-44 cartridge.) But the British convinced them to modify it to accept the .280 British, and promoted it to the Americans. Well, we weren't having any of it, and in the end FN had to beef up the FAL to accept the 7.62X51, and bring it out as a competitor to the prototype M14.

All to no avail. The fix was in. The Army fixed the tests, and in the end "proved" the M14 the superior rifle to the FAL.

The M14 was adopted in 1957, but production was slow. The problem was twofold: the M14 was sold as the best rifle to be had at the time, partly on the inexpensive change-over: the advocates promised that much of the M1 Garand tooling could be utilized to make M14s. Wrong. In the end, the manufacturers ended up producing all-new tooling just for the M14. Second, the peculiarities of the procurement system meant that not that many manufacturers were willing to risk their future on acquiring a government contract. One of the companies that was willing was TRW. You probably know of them as the credit report company, but back then they were a hi-precision manufacturing firm who made just about everything, from seat belt assemblies to rocket components. They sought out a contract for the M14, and approached it not as a firearm, but as a precision-made manufactured product.

Instead of rows each of lathes and mills, for example, they used early automated cutting machines. As a result, TRW made money on the M14, where other companies didn't. Not because they were so tight with a buck, or clever in making them inexpensively, but because they garnered the bonuses in the contract clauses for early delivery and quality control.

Then Secretary of Defense McNamara killed the Springfield Armory as a manufacturing site, and cancelled contracts, intending to re-bid. By then, the M16 was adopted (another story, and well-covered elsewhere) and the M14 was done. But not before being further enmeshed in controversy.

Despite being adopted in 1957, by the time of the Berlin Wall being erected (August 1961) the Berlin Brigade was still equipped with M1 Garands. As late as the end of 1962, the 101st Airborne was the only unit fully-equipped with M14s, the USMC Fleet Marines being the second unit. At that rate, it would have been sometime around the Bicentennial before the whole Army was switched over to the M14.

The Air Force, wishing to flex their muscle, wanted something besides cast-off M1 Carbines for the SAC guards who were standing guard over ready-to-go nuclear-armed bombers. That's right, the guys standing out in the rain, cold and wind, who were guarding nuke-armed B-52 bombers, were using M1 Carbines,. Worse yet, the maintenance and parts resupply of those carbines was handled by the Army. The Air Force wanted something under their own control. Buying M14s was not going to cut it, both because they were slow in being made, but also the Army would have controlled maintenance and supply. So the Air Force bought a small batch of AR-15 rifles. With that, the AR-15 suddenly became available in the government procurement system.

What with a shooting war heating up and erratic production of the M14, the Army had to have rifles. What they wanted was one of the new whiz-bang R&D rifles that were promised to be "almost ready" for them. What they had to do was buy rifles right now. Since the Air Force had bought AR-15 automatic rifles (the early production ARs were indeed marked "AR-15" but were select-fire, i.e., machineguns) and thus were "in the system" the Army, reluctantly, got talked into buying them as a stop-gap measure (and then footing the bill, in money and casualties, to de-bug the design).

Having bought a lightweight carbine for jungle warfare, the Army found itself short of sniper rifles. Not that the Army every really took a liking to snipers. In many quarters they were viewed with barely-hidden dislike.

Sniper rifles had been bolt-action rifles for a long time. The Army and Marines had used the M1C and M1D sniper rifles during WWII, but those were old, and the M14 was pressed into use. Combined with a ranging telescopic sight, the M21 worked well in Vietnam.

While the Army switched to the M16 in Vietnam, target shooters back home did not. The M16 of the early era was not at all suited to long-range target shooting. The 55-grain bullet is too light to carry well (wind drift and drop at range are beyond un-impressive) and the sights were not click-adjustable. So, the NRA High Power shooters continued to use the M14. At least, those who were not using the Garand. For a long time, there was a definite two-tier status/caste system in NRA High Power: the service teams, and those who could get an M14 on loan, used them. Everyone else used M1 Garands. And yes, you could get an M14 to shoot competition with, back then.

(True story: in the early 1980s, one of the guys in my gun club was in the NG, in a Ranger unit. Yes, there were Ranger National Guard units back then. The Army later turned all the NG units into truck drivers, but that's a different story. Paul managed to talk the Supply Sergeant into allowing him to check out an M16 for personal use. So, we ended up at the gun club

The M14 is a short-stroke piston system that is self-throttling and durable.

with all the .223 ammo we could find, to spend a day shooting a government-owned M16. It was not uncommon then. Today, it would be completely unheard of, and people would be imprisoned for doing it.)

By the mid-1990s, the AR-15 had been developed and refined to the point that it could compete on the 600 yard course of fire of NRA High Power. A 68-grain or heavier bullet, pushed to full velocity, in an accurized AR, was one-MOA to 600 yards.

But before then, the M1A came about. What with the M14 being mothballed, there were lots and lots of spare parts to be had. There had been a few other attempts, but a new company by the name of Springfield Armory began making the M1A in 1974. Competition shooters could have a semi-auto only copy of the M14, and once fully accurized it was just as good as the government models. As with all things, the supply of USGI parts dried up, and Springfield had to, over time, make or procure each of the parts as that supply ran out. However, with standards to uphold, each replacement was made to the same quality of the originals. (The snobbish might disagree, but cosmetics aside, the replacements are as good. They had to be, since they would be compared directly to the originals.)

As an aside, there were Springfield Armory-made M14s. Well, not real, actual USGI-accepted M14 rifles, but select-fire rifles of the M14 pattern. From the 1974 beginnings, until 1986, it was possible to order a select-fire M1A. The Hughes Amendment to FOPA 1986 banned production of new select-fire firearms. But the select-fire M1A is a rarity, as those who wanted an M1A usually wanted one for target shooting, not machine gun shooting.

What is a real screaming crime is the difference between a semi and an auto version: one little lug on the receiver. If you were to take an M14, slap it on a magnetic vise of a surface grinder, you could grind off the lug (a brief aside: doing so, while not a crime by Federal regs, would be a crime against the firearms community) and the result would differ in no way besides markings from a semi-auto receiver. However, the position of the government, via the BATFE, is "once a machine gun, always a machine gun." In any rational administration, in 1992, when the M14 was declared to finally be surplus, the smart thing to do would have been to grind off the lugs and sell them as surplus to

The M14, in an epoxy GI stock, with a Springfield Armory mount and Leupold scope, set up for sniping.

A member of the 101st provides cover in the mountains of Afghanistan. DoD photo by Pfc. Donald Watkins, U.S. Army.

law-abiding taxpaying citizens. Half a million rifles at only $500 each would have meant $250 million to the government coffers. Chump change to some, it would have paid for 100 M1A1 main battle tanks.

Since then, Springfield has refined the M1A to the point that they offer a model for just about any use or need.

## Springfield Armory

You can buy an M1A today. Not only a clone of a mil-spec rifle of the late 1950s, but modern ones as well, as evidenced by the SOCOM 16. The classic is just that, the classic. Everything you'd want, then or now. The SOCOM 16 is *sui generis*, genuinely one of a kind.

The originals had three things going against them, measured by today's standards: wooden stock, long barrel, no place to put extras. The wooden stock is easy. Once you have a mold made, you can pop out synthetic stocks left and right for the cost of the materials and labor. And since target shooters long-ago decided that plastic was superior to wood, synthetic stocks for the M1A/M14 have been in existence for a long time.

The second one is a bit different. The M14, as originally made, had a 22-inch barrel. That's right, 22 inches, and a flash hider nearly four inches long at the end of that. Why so much? Well, the end result was a rifle no longer than the one it was replacing, the M1 Garand. And if you wanted all the velocity you could get out of a 147-grain FMJ, and wanted to keep pressures under control, you needed a long barrel. The flash hider was a new development, and being new, probably not as well-engineered as we expect such things to be today. Not that it's bad, it's just long. With CAD/CAM design, and lots more experience, we could easily (and do) make a flash hider just as effective but shorter.

So Springfield Armory shortened the M1A barrel to 16 inches plus change, and installed a muzzle brake on the end. Rather than try to hide the flash, they decided to use the gases to dampen muzzle rise and recoil.

The SOCOM 16 uses a standard synthetic stock, with a block bolted to the barrel. The top handguard is slotted to provide clearance, and you can mount a red-dot scope on the rail on the barrel. Now, lots and lots of shooting will heat up the barrel and the block. This will probably cause a shift in point of aim, but that is not a

The Springfield Armory SOCOM 16, with the top rail, and a red-dot.

real problem. I mean, to reach that point, you'd have to either be on a ridgeline in Korea, right in the middle of the second Korean War, dealing with human wave assaults, or in the middle of the zombie apocalypse, and facing waves of fast-movers. In either instance, your problem will not be in point of impact/aim shift due to overheating, but two others: "do you have enough ammo?" and "who is going to reload your mags, if you can't stop shooting to do it yourself?"

However, to solve that problem, and provide an answer to the third shortcoming of the classic design, Springfield came up with the SOCOM II. The "II" takes the synthetic stock, and mounts a railed shell on the forearm of it. The red-dot gets mounted on the shell, and thus is removed from the barrel. The rails also provides plenty of room to mount lights, lasers, and whatever else you might want mounted.

In use, the M1A is identical to the M14, except for lacking the "giggle switch." To load, stuff the magazines full. M14 magazines are common, and even though the supply of surplus is getting old, replacement magazines are now appearing. To give you an idea of just how common they used to be, I had bought my M1A back when they were still being assembled from all-surplus parts. I needed extra magazines. (I bought it when the owner came into the store to sell. It came with two ammo cans full of ammo, and two ammo cans full of magazines. Of course I needed more mags.)

Soon after, a wholesaler had a sale on magazines. New, in the wrapper M14 magazines were $3.99. New, unwrapped; $2.99. New, used magazines were a whopping $1.99. I bought a footlocker of them. Through the years, when someone mentioned they needed mags, I'd say "I have a few" and sell off some. When I realized I was down to little more than a basic load, I stopped selling my "extras."

The magazine fits into the rifle the same way the AK and FAL do: lock and rock. Lock the front latch, and rock the magazine back to catch the rear latch. One aspect of the M14 that is nearly unique: it has a built-in magazine loader. The stripper clip guide on top allows you to stuff magazines full, while they are in the rifle.

Pull back the operating rod handle, let go, and you have a round in the chamber. The safety is the same as the Garand: stick a finger in the trigger guard, push the safety forward, and you're ready to go. Yes, they

The SOCOM II has plenty of rail estate where you can mount items such as this Insight ATPIAL.

had a different idea of safe back then. Pull the trigger, it shoots, one per.

Once empty, the bolt locks back. Remove the magazine by pressing the rear latch and rocking the magazine forward. Insert, yank the op rod, and repeat.

As I said, if you want the classic, you can have it. Or you can upgrade. Springfield also makes the Super Match, a rifle built for target competition. It has a heavy, air-gauged match barrel; the receiver is a special one with a lug at the rear so you can bolt it tightly to the stock. Or, you can have the M21, a copy of the Vietnam-era sniper rifle, with improvements since then. The stock, for one. Instead of a standard stock with a hand towel taped to it for proper cheek weld, you get a stock with an adjustable cheekpiece.

And if all that wasn't enough, Springfield will mix and match. Want a standard M1A with a synthetic camo stock? Done. Match with a railed handguard? Done. One aspect of the M1A that they used to do that I don't see anymore is calibers. It used to be that you could order up an M1A in .243 instead of .308. However, there are still plenty of gunsmiths who know how to build one. If you really, really want an M1A in something besides .308, find one of them. Discuss the cost of a replacement barrel. He probably has customers who would very much like a brand-new barrel from

Just so there is no doubt, Springfield marks the "II."

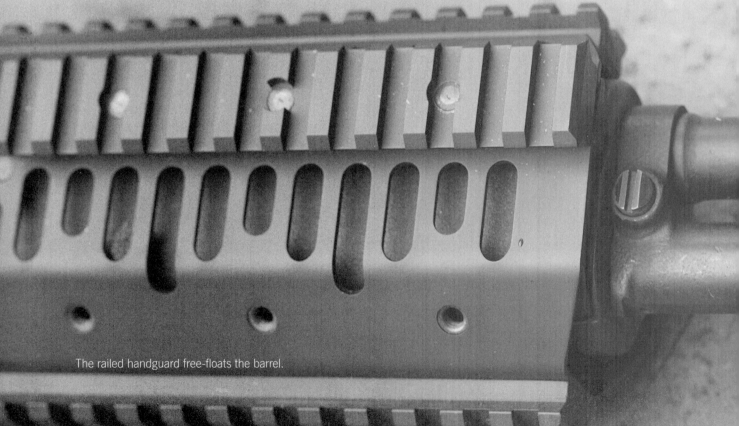

The railed handguard free-floats the barrel.

The muzzle brake takes a bit of recoil out of the SOCOM II, and makes it kosher for places that do not allow flash hiders.

Springfield, to replace their shot-out tube. And hey, Springfield may still have a few barrels lying around. Ask them.

## Iraq and Later

When we entered Iraq, we found that we needed semi-auto big bore rifles. The cry went out "get us M14s." Nice try, but way too late. We had few to none. And worse yet, we had no supply of spare parts, and no trained armorers. The parts had been scrapped or sold, and the trained armorers had retired. So we had re-re-re-built M14s, with the soldier using them having maybe three or four magazines, period (and no hope of ever getting more, unless the folks at home mail him some) and if anything broke, he was done. There simply were no rifles to be had, and no spares for them.

Which is why we are now seeing so many modern AR-10 rifles coming into the marketplace, to fill the niche of big-bore semi-auto sniper rifle. Not because we couldn't build more M14s. We could if we wanted to. But no-one in the services knows how to use anything but an M16 or M4, and it is easier to buy new .308

M16s than it is to buy M14s and then train everyone on how to use them.

## End of the Line

While the various producers manufactured over 1.3 million M14s before production was shut down in the early 1960s, we don't have many left. The simple attrition of four decades of use would account for some, but the bulk can be laid at the loafers of one William Jefferson Clinton. Soon after taking office, he ordered the destruction of surplus small arms instead of their sale through the DCM, now the CMP. So, over half a million functional M14s were de-milled for reasons that can only be described as venal, paranoid or politically retributive. Worse yet, they were not stripped for the spare parts, but the rifles, whole, were fed into shredders or stuffed into smelters. Those few M14s you see in photos in Iraq or Afghanistan are the rare survivors, and the soldiers, Marines and sailors who use them probably have no idea that what they are using are practically museum pieces, not because of their age, but because of their rarity.

If you have more gear than these rails can hold, you'd better eat your wheaties before picking up the "II."

**Chapter 5**

# Bullpups

n researching this book and this chapter, I came across an interesting tidbit: the first semi-auto bullpup designs were French, made during their semi-auto R&D phase during WWI. I shoulda known. The biggest push came after WWII, when the British proposed a bullpup called the EM2 and even made a bunch of test-fire prototypes.

I have seen one newsreel from the time of a demo for military officers, the press and apparently anyone else who cared to show up. (They did things differently then. Today it would be a closed demo, and only those with the ability to "green light" the spending money for it would get to see it.) The demo (and I must point out that not a single person there, not even the soldiers shooting the rifles, seemed to have anything in the way of hearing or eye protection) consisted of shooting from a prone supported rest at a target or targets. The rifles used were a Lee-Enfield No. 4, a Garand, and the EM2. The Enfield shooter managed 27 shots in a minute, the Garand 44, and the EM2 86. Now, that is some good shooting, to get 27 out of a bolt gun was some fast bolt-working. That meant he started with10, shot them, jammed two stripper clips full in, fired them, and two more chargers of five each, and got seven of those 10 off before time ran out. The Garand shooter started with eight, and managed to shoot and load five more en-bloc clips, finishing the time with four rounds unfired.

The EM2 shooter almost finished off five full magazines. However, keep in mind that the Enfield and Garand were full-power rifles: the .303 British and the .30-06 respectively. The EM2 shot (depending on which model they used) a 7mm bullet at something like 2500 fps. So recoil was reduced, and had they used any self-loading rifle, with a 20-round magazine and lower recoil, they might well have gotten as many shots off.

Bullpups require a slightly different manual of arms.

The EM2, which apparently never made it past the prototype stage, was pretty much the bullpup high spot for many decades. Those wishing to have a bullpup rifle wandered in the wilderness for a long time, but things did get better.

Today, bullpup-lovers never had it so good. Currently, we have the AUG in a host of models. There are the originals, the new one from Steyr, and the several replacements that have come about recently that use AR-15 magazines, and they all have adherents. There is the Kel-Tec RFB for the big-bore bullpup lovers. There are continuing rumors that the Israelis will export, or license the manufacture, of their Tavor TAR-21, but while the rumors persist, I have not yet seen any "in the flesh," at least not outside of demos and sample mockups.

The evergreen Bushmaster M17S is always looked at longingly by the bullpup fans, but it never seems to feel the love that other models do.

FNH-USA has their FS2000, a bullpup that (on paper anyway) has all the features you'd want: it takes AR mags, it ejects out the front, the handguard and top cover can be swapped out, and it comes from FN, always a good thing. But, it tends towards the porky side (sorry, FN, but true) and while it looks great in the photos, it always gives me that "ewww" feeling when I pick it up. If they slimmed it down, that would be something. It handles better than the first impression would lead you to believe, but it never (at least, not for me) ever warms up to "Hey, I like this."

There are the exotics, the rarities that you'd have to win the lottery to be able to buy: the French FAMAs (last I heard, going for $8000) and the "Cadet" version of the British SA80. (That one is the semi-auto-only version, one that qualified for import for about five minutes before various import restrictions kept it out. It would probably cost you more than a FAMAs would.)

You could call the FN P90 and/or PS90 bullpups, but you'd get some curious looks from the bullpup crowd. It is just a little too strange for their tastes to be accepted as a bullpup. And none of these even cover the many models (I've uncovered more than 50 designs) that are not currently being manufactured but are not allowed for importation, were made as prototypes, or are simply curiosities lurking in foreign arms museums. I'm certain, as I scour the museums of Europe, that one of these days I'm going to uncover a flintlock bullpup. Heck, I've already discovered several flintlock revolving rifles, so there had to be at least one bullpup, right? And if we delve back into the historical past, we even find bolt-action bullpups.

One of the aspects of the bullpup that hinders acceptance is the manual of arms – or rather, the changes in the accepted manual of arms, in order to accommodate the changed layout. You've got to change your habits (some of us have been doing this for decades, and changes do not come easily) and that means re-thinking how to do simple things. Like reloads: strong hand or weak hand? Do you keep your hand on the pistol grip and wrestle a magazine back there (nearly to your armpit) with the other, or do you let go of the pistol grip and snap one in more easily? Well, more easily for some of us. Add in web gear, or a tac vest, or body armor and the vest/web gear, and it really gets problematic.

**YOU'VE GOT TO CHANGE YOUR HABITS (SOME OF US HAVE BEEN DOING THIS FOR DECADES, AND CHANGES DO NOT COME EASILY) AND THAT MEANS RE-THINKING HOW TO DO SIMPLE THINGS.**

But it was a lot worse back in "the day." You see, the shooters who favored bullpups did not always have the wide array they have today. Back then, if you wanted a bullpup, and you could not afford one of the fabulous AUGs, you took the other way out: you made one. You took an existing rifle, and you placed it into a polymer clamshell, and the shell held things in place to "create" a bullpup rifle. One of the samples can be seen in the (mostly execrable) movie *Starship Troopers*. Besides trashing a great novel, and killing or at least stalling the careers of a number of actors, it featured Mini-14 rifles inside of bullpup clamshell adapters. Now, companies still make this kind of shell, for the Mini and other rifles, but it really isn't a good idea. (And the movie is almost bad enough to be a real popcorn-fest of a hoot-at-it-and-snort flick. Almost.)

One drawback is the rear-mounted magazine. It might interfere with gear you've strapped on. If you change rifles, check your gear.

The original FAL, a Para model, and the RFB. The RFB is as compact as the Para with its stock folded. However, the Para with the stock folded is a big "pistol" and the RFB is a rifle the sights of which you can actually use.

Why is the clamshell approach not a good idea? First of all, the operating handle is in the wrong place, second the balance is off, third your face is not protected from mishaps, and as the *piece de resistance* the triggers really suck. But the biggest thing is simply this: such compromises entail some really awkward details. One shell I looked at some years ago was literally that: two shells, held together with a fistful of screws. You had to screw a dozen fasteners tight to enclose the mechanism inside the two halves. And when you shot it, they worked loose, each in its own time, and had to be tightened up on a regular basis. You couldn't use some sort of thread fastener, because the screws threaded into plastic. And even if they were bushed with brass liners, you'd have to take them out to clean it.

Others used fewer screws, but the two halves had lips that had to be caught/interwoven, one under the other. Squeeze it too tightly, or (as happened to one shooter I saw, in an early 3-gun match) fall on it and the whole thing springs apart. Invariably, the adapter shells fit poorly, with the mechanism either rattling around loose inside, or being trapped and binding. Plastic under stress is not happy plastic, and stress can lead to premature failure.

Also, the loose fit is not conducive to good accuracy. Barrels being stressed, or actions rattling around inside the shell while your sights or scope are mounted to the shell itself, do not lead to good results. The loose shells also make trigger pulls even more of a problem. The linkage has to take into account the slop in the fit, and so you can end up with a literal inch of take-up in the trigger pull before the linkage finally makes contact with the existing trigger. Not that the folks who make the shells don't try, and try hard. But the adaptations needed to get a rifle that originally wasn't a bullpup into a bullpup configuration are just too much. At least they are for me.

Many have tried them, and if everyone found them unsuited, there wouldn't be any companies left. Such is the power of market-driven design.

There is another aspect to the clamp-on adapter stocks, and that is sights and optics. A rifle designed from the ground up (or "starting with a clean sheet of paper" for those who are collecting out-of-date metaphors) will have the stock located, and the sights arranged such, that they are usable. Or not there at all, but with provisions for them. The original AUG is one, where the carry handle was the optical sight. The new AUG and the Kel-Tec RFB are others featuring no sights but have a long rail located where you need it.

The clamp-together systems have sights on stalks. They have the problem of the original mechanism having been designed for a regular stock, and the sights have to be high enough to see. Combine that with the short sight radius, and you have tall sights that look like your thumb out there. No, I mean it: fat sights have a short sighting radius and are hard to use.

The optics problems come about from the cantilevered nature of the stock designs. To get the optics located where you can use them, they have to be out over the barrel. But to get a rail there you practically have to enclose the length of the barrel in a tube or other structure. Make the tube/rail strong enough to be rigid, and it is heavy. Or bulky. Make it slimmer and it flexes and your zero wanders.

Of all the designs that have been wrestled into the bullpup configuration, the AK has to be the most unsuited, which is why I'm always surprised when I'm reminded that the Chinese have invested a lot of R&D and PR effort into their new rifle. (And with a new caliber, too.) To add to the adaptation woes of the bullpup-in-a-clamshell, the AK design also adds the safety lever.

Now, I've said it before, and I'll say it again: I'm not a fan of bullpups. I recognize that there are advantages to the bullpup design, but I don't think anyone has come up with one that really makes it advantageous. Yes, there are improvements, but they do not add up to enough to outweigh the advantages and inertia of the existing rifles. And that is the crux: anyone coming out with something new has to prove that it is not just better, but enough better to permit the old order to be overthrown.

An example is one that comes from the AR-verse, and I have sworn not to discuss ARs in this book – at least not much. Consider the Magpul PMag30. Yes, people had made polymer magazines before. But they had not been enough better than the existing magazines that shooters would consider ditching their existing magazines for the new ones. When someone comes up with a bullpup design that has all the advantages, and minimizes or eliminates the awkward parts, then they will have a smoking-hot product on their hands. And the clamshell adaptations are far from smoking-hot.

After all this, you're probably wondering why I don't have any of the shells to show you. Well, I thought I did. However, the secret hidden bunker here at Gun Abuse Central is stuffed. So stuffed, that I almost got buried in a gear-alanche while looking for the bullpup stock I knew was in there.

Kel Tec RFB

Now, if you are just lusting for a bullpup, you have to have one, what should you do? Go out and plop down $1,000 to $2,000 on a rifle? Maybe, maybe not. Even in times when rifles are selling, and selling briskly, you're going to lose money if you find out a bullpup just isn't for you. Worse yet, if you buy at the market peak, find out it isn't for you, and have to sell at the trough, you could lose half your investment or more. What you should do, is follow the advice I've given on many other subjects and many other occasions: go to the nearest USPSA club, one that holds 3-gun matches, and become a member. There, you'll get to see what works and what doesn't. You'll get to talk to those who shoot, and shoot a lot, and find out what survives.

And, once you get known, you'll have chances to try other member's rifles. With just a little bit of luck you'll find the resident club members who are bullpup fanatics, and they will be more than happy to let you have a go. After all, if they "convert" you, you'll be one more in their merry little band. You might well find yourself shooting rarities that you cannot afford, just "because you have to try this one." If all it costs you is ammo, it will be educational, and perhaps money-saving as well.

If you have a burning desire for a bullpup, don't let me stop you. Go out and find one. There is too little happiness in the world to deny you that experience. Just don't ask me to lust for one, not yet.

French soldiers from the 27th Alpine Rangers Battalion and French Task Force Tiger patrol the valleys of Kapisa province, Afghanistan, April 21, 2009. DoD photo by Maj. Patrick Simo. PD-USGOV-MILITARY.

Chapter 6

# The Kel-Tec RFB

Having just told you how much I am cool to bullpups, the Kel-Tec RFB is the one that may well break my personal preference for regular rifles. Kel-Tec is a manufacturer that apparently has a design philosophy unlike that of other firearms companies: they want their firearms to look business-like and industrial – which, to my mind and eye, is a good thing. As much as I love a classic walnut stock on a pre-64 Winchester 70, on rifles meant for business, it isn't so good.

The Kel-Tec RFB (Rifle, Forward-ejecting Bullpup) has as its heart an FAL action. But that is just a thumbnail description and doesn't do justice to the extra work they had to do to get things the way they wanted. First of all, the standard FAL action has a long tube down the stock, holding the recoil spring. To make a bullpup you have to move that. So, the RFB is not merely an FAL action, but a para-stocked FAL, the folder. Of course, since the stock ends at the back of the action, there is no stock to fold, but you'd expect that.

Second, they dealt with the main problem many bullpups have, of ejection. If you'll remember previously, ejecting out the side makes a bullpup non-ambidextrous. So, the RFB, instead of hurling the brass out the side, grabs each empty (and live ones you manually eject) and pulls them to the side, stuffing them into a tube leading toward the muzzle.

It is startling at first to shoot an RFB on the bench, and when you go to move it to the rack to check the targets, to have the brass from your rounds scoot out of the tube, onto the ground.

Not only do you not have to worry about ejection, but in the instance of a case failure, your face being right on top of the action isn't a problem. Kel-Tec designed it so there are two sheets of steel between your face and the action, each 1.6mm thick.

Even I, a bullpup-disliker, find the RFB a real smooth operator.

There is no reason bullpups can't be accurate. The RFB definitely is accurate.

The empties are extracted and then stuffed into a tube that dumps them out near the muzzle.

The top rail allows for all kinds of optics.

The FAL action inside is a metric FAL, so you'll need metric magazines to feed it. This is fine, because in the list of readily-available magazines, metric FAL are near the top. Unlike a regular FAL, where you rock the magazines in, the RFB has its magazines sliding inline, just like an AR magazine.

The ergonomics of the pistol grip and forearm are stupendous. In many instances of a bullpup design, the forearm is either as fat as a pregnant walrus cow or nonexistent. The RFB has normal, even comfortable, dimensions on both of these. The safety lever is ambidextrous, and this leads me to the biggest leap forward that Kel-Tec has engineered into the RFB: the trigger. Most bullpup designs, because of the need to have linkage between the trigger (which is 'way forward of where it would normally be) and the action, have triggers that rate high on the suck-o-meter. In some cases, you can feel the parts flexing and bending as you apply more and more pressure, until the thing finally deigns to fire. Not so the RFB. The trigger is clean, crisp and while not the lightest, certainly light enough. That alone is reason enough to consider it, even if everything else were lacking, which it isn't.

The RFB works with all my .308 gear.

The safety also disconnects the trigger from the linkage and blocks the hammer, so it is drop-safe.

At just over eight pounds for the carbine (18-inch barrel, 26 inches overall) and a little over 11 pounds for the long-barrel version (32 inches!) the RFB is not a featherweight. It also isn't a portly toad. The compact carbine, with a scope or red-dot (it does not come with iron sights) and a loaded magazine and sling, weighs less than a comparably-equipped M14/M1A or AR-10.

The charging handle is up front, and the lever can be moved from one side to the other, as you wish. The top of the rifle features a long rail, where you'd park a red-dot optic or scope. You probably could put back-up iron sights up there, but as the rail is rather short for that sort of thing, they would be emergency-use only. Then again, the whole idea of a BUIS is emergency use.

With bullpups, you have to reload in new ways.

In firing, it is no big deal. Once you get it to your shoulder you have no idea if it is a bullpup or not, and things proceed normally. Well, for most of you it will, but me, not so much. My abnormal grip once again gave me problems. You see, I choke up on a grip like there's no tomorrow. This puts my trigger finger, or the base of it, in line with the leading edge of the safety lever. Each time I shoot, the lever comes back and nudges my trigger finger. Or rather, the rifle itself moves in my hands, enough to let the safety lever kiss my hand. Over time this becomes a bit less than fun. So, were I to spend a lot of time with an RFB, I'd have to relieve that edge. Since Kel-Tec probably would not want me modifying a loaner, I didn't do that, and simply put up with the kissing.

The barrel is capped with an A2-style flash hider

Not all the ways to reload a bullpup allow for keeping your hand on the pistol grip.

(clearly, the threads differ from an AR, otherwise there could be trouble) and are the standard .308 5/8x24 tpi so you can replace the A2 if you really, really need to have something else.

I did not find any ammo that the RFB did not work with. I'm sure there will be some, as no rifle works with everything that is made, but I haven't found any yet.

I first saw the RFB at the SHOT Show where Kel-Tec had a prototype on display. The prototype, as an engineering model, was fine. But it was not at all as handsome as the production rifle. If you want a .308 rifle, this bears consideration. If you want a bullpup, this is certainly one to watch. If you have to have both, stop looking. Here it is.

**Chapter 7**

# The Steyr AUG

The Armee Universal Gewehr, or Universal Army Rifle (AUG), sprang onto the scene in 1977, when it replaced the StG 58, the Austrian-made copy of the FAL. Called (no great surprise here) the StG 77, the AUG was impressive in the technological advances that were wrapped into one package.

First off, it is a bullpup, which made it the cause célèbre of the tactical set, in the late 1970s and early 1980s. Bullpups were the wave of the future, if we old Neanderthals would just rub the mastodon fat out of our eyes and see the rightness of the bullpup cause. Snarkiness aside, it was a big advance.

First, the receiver was a steel alloy casting, finish-machined, and then enclosed in a polymer shell. The receiver also held the sights, which on the original was a 1.5X Swarovski Optik scope, with a central "pip" and a ring around the center dot. For close and fast use, the circle was plenty good enough. If you needed precision, then using the dot in the center as your aiming point got you the hits you needed.

The scope was not an extra, bolted to the receiver; it was machined as the carry handle, an integral part of the receiver. As such, it was a lot sturdier than your usual scope setup back in 1977. Of course, the obvious drawback is that if the handle gets bent, you have to either scrap the receiver, or send it back to an armorer's station sufficiently equipped (usually the factory) to heat and bend it back.

The barrel is another big advance. You see, removing the barrel is simply a matter of locking the bolt back, pressing a lever to the side, and pulling the barrel out the front. If you want to replace it with another, install the new one, lock it (the latch closes and locks automatically) and you're done. You'd have to re-zero for a re-placement barrel, but so what? With an inventory of rifles and receivers, and a rack of barrels, you can make them short or long, as needed by the end-users. Of course, every time you swap barrels you have to re-zero, but no-one who is at all serious about what they do takes a rifle out of the rack and uses it without checking the zero, anyway.

The flash hider/comp is quite effective, as the hair on my arms can attest. This shot is captured at the moment the gases hit the comp.

The AUG magazines are heavy-duty plastic, and you can see the rounds inside

The empties are tossed to the side, without muss, fuss or mangling.

The barrel swap advantage also means that worn barrels can be replaced at whatever level unit the authorities deem appropriate, and not just at an armorer's shop, with the benches, vise and tools to change barrels, as in the AR-15.

The radical appearance of the AUG also meant it was a natural for the movies. It has appeared in movies as good as *Die Hard* and as bad as *Harley Davidson and the Marlboro Man*.

The polymer shell that holds the parts is composed of flat curves, if you follow. The large, flat-ish areas mean few nooks and crannies to collect dirt, dust, lint and other gunk from the field, and this make it easy to clean. Heck, if you really had to clean a passle of AUGs quickly, you could strip the receivers and trigger packs from the shells and power-wash the shells down at the quarter car wash.

The trigger pack is likewise composed of polymer, although he chemical composition of it is different, as it is a bit harder than the shell enclosing the rest of things. One big change the Austrian designers of the AUG added was a lack of select fire. Not as in "semi-automatic only" but as in no selector lever. For military use, the designers instead came up with a trigger pack that offered "clutch" auto fire. If you wanted to fire a single shot, you simply squeezed the trigger as you would in correct target-shooting manner. If you wanted full-auto fire, you snatch the trigger back quickly. If you snatch it quickly enough, the trigger pack overrides the disconnector, and full-auto fire ensues. Let go,

Some AUG clones use AR mags, but the real-deal new version uses the originals.

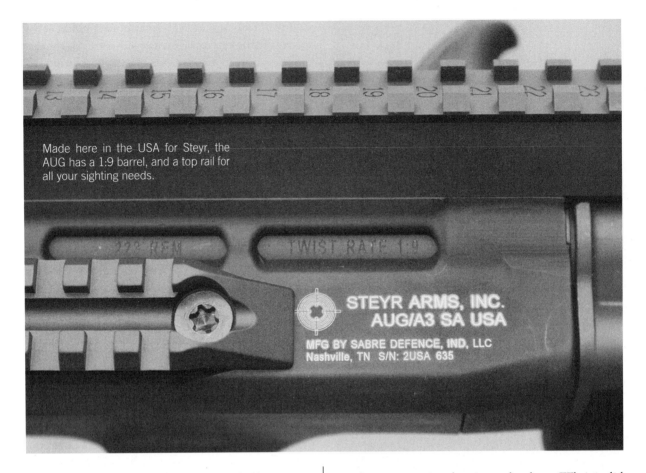

Made here in the USA for Steyr, the AUG has a 1:9 barrel, and a top rail for all your sighting needs.

STEYR ARMS, INC.
AUG/A3 SA USA

MFG BY SABRE DEFENCE, IND, LLC
Nashville, TN  S/N: 2USA 635

and the mechanism re-sets, and you're back to semi-auto on a careful press, and have to snatch it to resume full-auto fire.

Now, this outraged the purists. The idea was that when needed, the soldier would be snatching the trigger anyway, and thus get the full-auto fire desired. We've since found that one can actually aim full-auto or burst fire. Yes,

The muzzle brake works quite well and is low-profile.

you have to practice, but it can be done. What it did do, was make the AUG a rare and wondrous thing, for not many back in the period from 1977 to 1986 could acquire a machinegun. Many states were huffy, or simply didn't allow it. Now, many more do, but the pesky Hughes Amendment makes them prohibitively expensive. There was a variant. The original was the AUG A1, and the semi-only version was the AUG SA. It, however, was banned in 1989 by then-President Bush (future history will probably call him "Bush the First") in a disgraceful fit of bipartisan equipment-blaming. Not many made it in, and as a result it is one of the few semi-auto rifles that costs nearly as much as the full-auto variant from which it was derived.

So, enter the Steyr AUG/A3 SA USA, a name nearly as long as the stubby little rifle itself. There have been

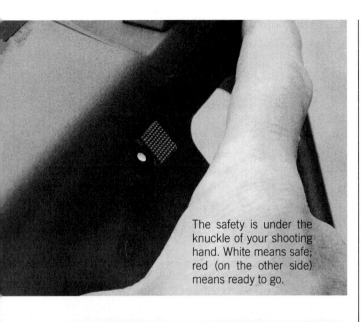

The safety is under the knuckle of your shooting hand. White means safe; red (on the other side) means ready to go.

The gas regulator. Leave it alone.

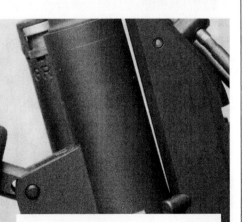

The vertical foregrip can be folded. Just pull down and pivot.

other companies who have built clones, before Steyr could get back into the US market. But things have changed since 1977, and the rifle has changed as well.

First, and most obviously, the handle/optic is gone. We have long since entered the era where the end-user selects the desired optic and refuses to be saddled with what the manufacturer deems is best. So, the receiver, while being the same basic forging/casting (Steyr is close-mouthed about it, but we can guess) has the handle gone, and in its place is a picatinny rail. The rail runs the length of the receiver, and is an integral part of it, not bolted on. My guess is that the receiver starts out as an investment casting, and is finish-machined to get the critical parts dead-on for location, size and direction. I've had some suggest that the receivers originally were forgings, but the thought of drilling the guide rod holes, were I a production manager, gives me the willies.

Unlike Sauron's Ring, one rail does not rule them all, so there is a second, accessory rail on the right side of the receiver. That's where you'd park a light, laser or your Ipod. If you need to install a laser targeting designator, such as an AN/PEQ2-A, you'll have to put it on the top rail, and use a scope or other optic that looks over it. There just isn't enough room on the side rail for such things, at least not until they get a lot smaller. Even an Insight ATPIAL (Advanced Target Pointer/ Illuminator/ Aiming Light) is too large, and those things are quite compact.

Currently in black, instead of the gray or green the originals were in, the polymer would probably take paint only reasonably well. Then again, if the idea is to camo your rifle, you don't want paint that sticks well. A weathered rifle is even more hidden.

The folding foregrip is the same, and when it is folded up it works as a regular forearm. The flash hider of the originals is gone. That one was a three-prong, open-slots design that worked fine, but doesn't pass muster in the modern era. To make the AUG marginally more accepted in some jurisdictions, it comes with a flash hider/muzzle brake that works better as a brake than a hider. (Most such compromises do just that; brake more than hide.) In shooting, I found the brake was effective, but since the muzzle is so close (it is a bullpup, after all) my arms could feel the blast.

The originals used a non-AR magazine designed by Steyr for the AUG. Made of a tough translucent plastic, you can, in good light, see how many rounds it holds. The originals were offered in 20-, 30- and 42-round capacity. Later clones of the AUG were made to accept AR-15 magazines, as those are common as dirt, and the supply of original AUG magazines that came in with the original rifles had not been augmented in decades. That made them quite expensive. Well, the new AUG is made for the old-style mags, and a new supply of the old-style magazines is now available. You get two with your rifle, and there are plenty in stock for those who want to load up. They work in the original rifles, too, for those lucky enough to have one.

The magazine inserts just like an AR's: straight up into the mag well. The big lever behind the magazine is the release button, and AUG magazines do not fall free. Hey, since you have to reach back there and press the button anyway, you might as well grab the magazine and pull it out, right? This is all in line with European tastes in such things: magazines are to be saved, re-loaded and reused, not strewn about the landscape to be picked up later.

The safety is a cross-bolt plastic bar above and behind the trigger. The white dot is safe, i.e., "it won't fire" and the red dot is fire, "this thing will hurt someone." You can easily use the base of your trigger finger to press the crossbar from safe to fire.

The trigger is the old semi-auto only trigger. That is, it doesn't matter how hard you clutch it, it isn't going to switch over into full-auto mode. Which is not a problem for me, as when I've had a chance to use the originals, I found the "trigger-snatch" to full-auto fire not at all fun, or useful. Oh well, tastes differ.

Now, the original was a big step forward. It was adopted by a number of countries, one of them being Australia, who were so taken with it that they licensed its manufacturer in Australia, so they would not have to depend on overnight shipments if they needed more. Called the A88, it apparently caused quite an uproar. The lower recoil of the 5.56, combined with the optical sight, improved rifle scores. Previously Australia had been using Australian-made FALs, in .308. Going from iron sights and .308 to optics and 5.56, it wasn't long before an embarrassingly large percentage of the Australian Army had posted scores on the qual course that equaled or exceeded those of the finest target competitors using L1A1 (FAL) rifles. The thresholds for Marksman, Expert, etc. had to be re-calculated and raised considerably.

Before we get to the shooting, let's take a turn about the beast, and see how it comes apart.

To unload, or check status, make sure that the safe-

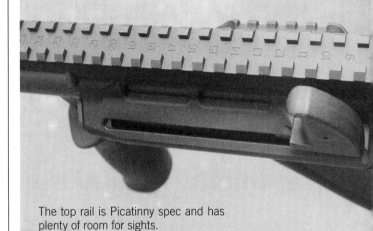

The button underneath is for the barrel removal. You have to have the bolt locked back to change the barrel.

The top rail is Picatinny spec and has plenty of room for sights.

Push the button to unlock the barrel.

When the barrel is unlocked, it pops forward, easy to remove.

Once out, the barrel is easy to clean.

ty is on and the white dot shows on the right. Remove the magazine. Grab the charging handle and haul it to the rear, and then tip it in towards the receiver. Tipping it up holds it open. You can now look inside and see if there are any rounds still lurking in there. See the button on the bottom front left of the receiver? Hold the foregrip, and press that button with the thumb of your left hand. It will pivot out of the

The receiver, the heart of the AUG.

way, and when it does, you can re-move the barrel. Just pull it forward and out. Now, grab the charging handle and lever it out from the receiver, but hold on to it and ease it forward.

Look at the middle of the shell. There is a flat, square button that looks like the safety but is much farther back, back near the magazine well. Press that from the left to the right. You'll have to push it halfway, and when your finger runs out of room, reach over and pull it the rest of the way. Be careful, because this locks the receiver into the shell, and when it comes loose the recoil springs will try to launch it out of the shell, onto the ground in front of you.

Once the receiver and bolt assembly are out, you simply grab the back of the bolt assembly and pull it out of the receiver to the rear. Before we go on, let's take a moment to look at what is in your hands right now.

The barrel has a lug on the front, with a cap on it. That is your gas adjustment, where you can set it to either run, run harder, or have no gas fed to it, for

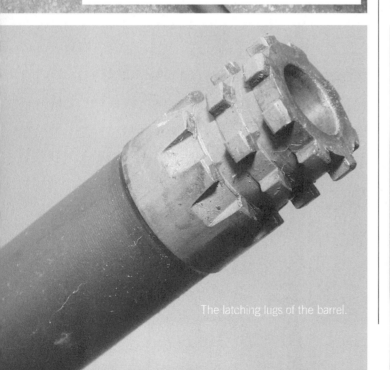

When you unlatch it for disassembly, the receiver tries to launch itself out of the shell.

The latching lugs of the barrel.

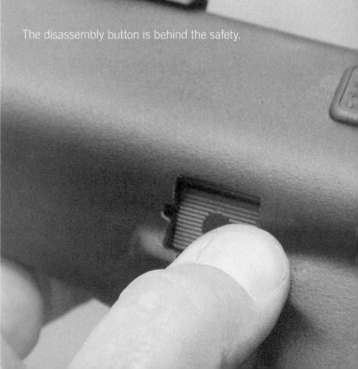

The disassembly button is behind the safety.

launching rifle grenades. Now, if you have an ample supply of rifle grenades to practice with or use, then this lever will be a source of fun. If not (like most of us) it is simply a knob you check to make sure it isn't in the wrong position and thus cause trouble. So, leave it alone. Yes, someone will point out that if you don't remove and clean it now and then, it will get carbon-welded in place. Good, I say, that way it can't be moved

The carrier has two guide rods.

and cause problems. As for the harsh-conditions setting, the one that feeds more gas to the system, again: leave it alone. When the Austrians are thinking "harsh conditions" they don't mean you and your buddies have spent an afternoon plinking on the back 40, hosing tin cans with merry abandon. No, that's just a bit grubby. By "harsh conditions" they mean something like being on the Eastern Front in wintertime, not having cleaned either the rifle

Here it is, all taken down for cleaning. Except for the trigger mechanism.

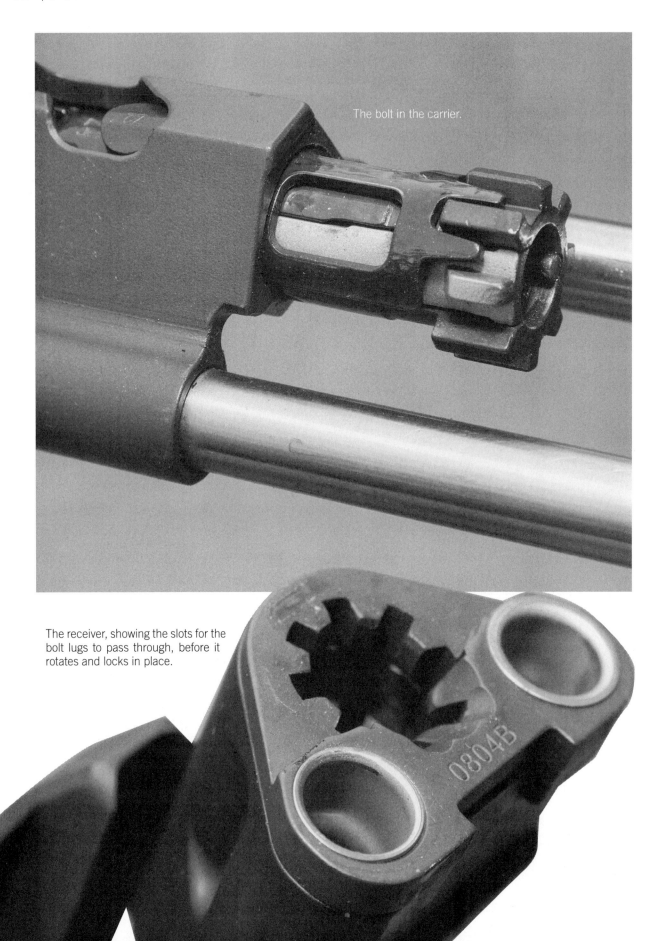

The bolt in the carrier.

The receiver, showing the slots for the bolt lugs to pass through, before it rotates and locks in place.

Press hard to take out the sling swivel, and then the buttplate

Here you see how the sling swivel is kept in place.

or yourself for a couple of weeks, and lost count of the distance you've crawled through mud and snow, and how many commies/zombies you've shot.

You aren't going to approach anything close to "harsh conditions" by their standards. Leave the gas setting alone.

Where were we? Oh yes, the barrel. To clean it, you simply pull a cleaning rod (brush, then patch) through the bore. Me, I'd pull from chamber to muzzle, but it hardly matters. Done.

The receiver, which you've pulled from the shell, has two major components: the housing, and the bolt and rails/rods assembly. The housing is a chunk of steel that holds the Picatinny rails, and contains the locking lugs for the bolt and barrel. The receiver is the real stumbling block to making the

AUG, or a clone of it. Let's take as an example the M-14/M1A, or the M1 Garand. To ensure correct headspacing, you have to closely control three variables: the rear of the lugs, the face of the bolt, and the shoulder of the chamber. Some might argue that the face of the receiver and the shoulder of the barrel, where they tighten up to each other, is another, but that is only if you are going to make barrels as a separate item, in a different location. Otherwise, it is a secondary item of manufacture.

On the AR-15, you have to control four variables: the bolt lug rear, the bolt face, the chamber shoulder,

The mostly plastic trigger housing and mechanism.

and the barrel extension lugs on their front faces.

The AUG requires that you track and control six dimensions: the bolt lugs' rear, the bolt face, the receiver locking lugs' front, the barrel locking lugs' front, the receiver barrel lug inserts' front, and the shoulder of the chamber. That's six detailed dimensions. Now, consider that the common "spread" allowed for correct head-spacing is .006". That means each of your six variables cannot waver more than a thousandth of an inch and still allow the assembly to come together correctly.

In reality, it means you have to hold tighter than that. So, who wants to make barrels (the easy part, probably) where the barrel lugs and chamber shoulder have to be on-dimension or wander not more than half a thousandth? That's right, not many.

On the bolt assembly, note that the bolt rotates using a cam pin, just as it does on the AR-15. However, since the cam pin is not controlled by the receiver, it would flop about if not directed. So, Steyr directed it. The bolt is spring-loaded in the forward position. Note the sheet metal "cage" with the fingers pointing forward. That

keeps the bolt lined up correctly. When the bolt goes forward into the receiver (inside the shell, of course) the fingers are pushed back, and the cam pin can then rotate the bolt to lock it to the receiver. That is correct, the bolt locks to the receiver, not directly to the barrel. That's how the barrel can be so slender.

On the back of the shell, you'll see the buttplate of the AUG. It appears to be, and is, a soft rubber plate. See the depression in it? Press that in, hard, with your thumb. While holding it there, yank the sling swivel out to the side. You can now remove the buttplate. Note the clips on the side. Those are what held onto the sling swivel post. The two, working together, kept the rear of the rifle assembled.

You can now pull the trigger assembly out of the rear of the rifle. It is a self-contained unit, and your first glance is correct: it is composed of plastic parts. The springs that drive things are steel, as are some of the pivot pins. But the housing and the parts themselves are plastic. Notice the mold marks on some of them? When I was in a class at Gunsite many years ago, I learned the

Yes, even the sear and hammer are plastic

The bolt, sliding into the receiver.

The mag well has the latch at the rear.

correct way to do a trigger job on an AUG: you carefully scrape the mold marks flush, and "lube" the trigger pack with an aerosol, non-wet Teflon lubricant. You don't want any normal lube in there where it can attract dirt, grit and gunk, and grind on the parts.

When you go to fire the AUG, if you hold a rifle at all as I do, you'll notice muzzle blast being re-directed by the flash hider. My arms felt a gentle, warm breeze from the flash. The 1:9 barrel shot all the ammo I had, and accurately enough to be called an accurate rifle. The trigger, with its plastic-on-plastic movement, doesn't help, but it isn't as much of a hindrance as I recall the AUGs I shot from the earlier era. Maybe they have worked on that detail, and maybe I just remember it differently. The magazines do not drop free, and you have to wrestle each of them out to reload.

The bullpup lovers and the AUG lusters will go ga-ga over it, but not me. While I admire the excellent engineering that went into it, and appreciate the clever barrel swap option, it just doesn't fit me, or the way I shoot. That, however, does not mean it is wrong for you. Only you can tell that.

Plenty accurate.

**Chapter 8**

# The FN SCAR

The Army has been trying to replace the M16 even before it adopted it. When the writing was on the wall back in the 1960s and the M14 was destined to be replaced, the Army immediately began searching for the future weapon that would slay all before it. They rapidly went through the SPIW, a combination grenade launcher and flechette spitter (the combo would make a comeback, later) burst-firing, multiple bullet loads, then later caseless cartridges, followed by the OICW, a "smart" grenade launcher. The Army, being the Army, is still at it, nearly 50 years later. And, being the Army, they have sorrowfully neglected the M16/M4 for pretty much all this time.

That may change. When we raced into and through Iraq and started hiking around Afghanistan, we entered a phase that the Army had not seen for several generations: sustained combat operations, where more than just the front-line grunts were involved. In WWII, it was not unusual to find company commanders (captains) and battalion commanders (majors) walking around with rifles because they needed them. Even with portable radios, the best and fastest way for the commander to get the info he needed was to be right up front.

Today, while a company commander may well be walking in a patrol with his men, he is often a slave of the radio, laptop and other comm gear. But, he'll have a rifle, because he needs it. Between then and now, not so much. It would have been a rare company commander in Vietnam who was packing a rifle and a full basic load of ammo. And for the non-Vietnam altercations we've been in, even less so.

So several generations of infantry officers not only got into the habit of not packing a long-gun, but were socially discouraged from carrying a rifle. The Army qualifications requirements were no help here, either. Lieutenants were issued rifles and expected to post a qualifying score. Captains were issued rifles if their job called for it, but didn't have to shoot. And above captain, no one was required to demonstrate any proficiency with any weapon whatsoever.

Worse yet, promotion boards looked at things such as schools attended ("Hmmm, no Master's degree? That Major will not do well on the coming 'boards'"), degrees gained, staff and command positions successfully held – but nothing to do with weapons.

Well, there are a whole lot more officers who are a lot more attuned to rifles today. And so we have a renewed interest in rifles, so much so that the Army, through SOCOM, is entertaining the thought of a new rifle. That rifle? The FNH-USA SCAR.

The biggest problems with the M16 are (to listen to its detractors, anyway) that it doesn't have a piston, and it's chambered in 5.56. So when it came time to design a new combat rifle, FNH decided to do a John Garand: they made one in two calibers. (For those who don't remember, when the M1 rifle was being proposed as the new service rifle, it was to be chambered in .276 Pedersen. John Garand, clever fellow that he was, figured that in the depression era a new cartridge was not going to be adopted. So he made prototypes of his finished product in both .276 Pedersen and .30-06. Sure enough, the Army loved the rifle, but the Chief of Staff; Douglas MacArthur – yes, that one – insisted that it be made in .30-06, not .276 Pedersen.)

FNH designed the SCAR to have commonality of parts between a 5.56 version and a 7.62 NATO version. The result is a rifle that looks a bit odd to those who become accustomed to a "rifle" being an M16/AR-15.

The original safety on the select-fire version had to be redesigned.

The bolt carrier is a marvel of design and engineering simplicity.

Before we can really discuss how it is different, we have to see just what-all there is on and on it.

First off, unlike the AR, on the SCAR the upper is the firearm, the portion that receives the serial number. Alongside the receiver there are six torx-head screws, a pair in the rear and one up front, on each side. These are the screws that hold the barrel in. Want to change barrels? Unbolt the screws (after you've disassembled it, of course) yank the barrel out, plug the new one in and tighten the screws. On top of the receiver is a full-length rail, where the back-up iron sights are parked. Well, the rear is; the front is on the barrel. So, like a properly-designed machine gun, with quick-change barrels, you can have the barrels for your SCAR pre-zeroed, and changing from one to the other does not affect your zero much, if at all.

The lower (and much of the rest of the rifle) is composed of polymer, and while the magazine well of the

The lower is not the rifle, the upper is. The lower is merely a polymer housing that holds the magazines and fire control parts.

SCAR-L, the 5.56 version, accepts standard AR-15 magazines, the internals are not at all like those of an AR. The trigger, safety, etc. are newly designed for the rifle, and don't look anything like the AR-15 internals we've become accustomed to. Hey, it's a new rifle – why should FNH restrict themselves to the old design?

The safety lever moves in the same way as the AR's, but to go from safe to semi is only an eighth of a turn, not a quarter. Push the safety all the way down (where "semi" would be on an M16/M4) and you have full-auto or burst. When I've used select-fire SCARs in competition, I had to make sure I kept a firm control over my thumb. Pushing past semi to full would be a

The bolt is very reminiscent of the AR-15, but better, with a massive extractor.

Recoil, as you would expect, is minimal.

The fire control parts are not at all like those of the AR-15/M16, and we'll all have to get used to something new.

The .308 SCAR uses an FAL-derived magazine.

Being piston driven, the SCAR has no functioning problem being turned into an SBR.

And yes, it shoots more than well enough to shoot another passing score.

At the FNH-USA 3-Gun championships, getting ready to shoot the SCAR-L in the mud.

good way to earn either a procedural, or get DQ'd from a match. (It would depend on the match rules.)

The stock both folds and has an adjustable cheekpiece. The cheekpiece clicks up or down, to position your face properly for either iron sights or a scope or to adjust if you have a fat face or a skinny one.

Inside, the action is a long-stroke piston, with a rotating barrel that looks like an AR-15 bolt, but no doubt with the metallurgical and coatings treatments that the Army refuses to adopt for the M16. The bolt carrier itself is also intriguing. It appears to simply be a flat, L-shaped block, with the bolt in the face of the leg of the L, and the long arm as the piston. The first time I looked at it, I realized that FNH engineers and designers had given themselves an edge. You see, with the carrier shaped that way, they can simply cut it from plate stock. Using (and this is just a guess, FNH hasn't let me watch) pre-hardened plates, they can surface-grind them dead flat, then use a high-pressure water jet to cut the outline of the carrier. Given the fine control of CNC machines, and the thin slot cut by the water jet, the machining left to do on the plate would be minimal, and a CNC machining station should be able to

The original models were done in flat dark earth. The commercial (semi-auto) version is first available in black.

In the match, they gave us a few shooting platforms that got us up out of the mud.

whip right through it. No castings or forgings to deal with, no complex curved surfaces, all easy and straight except for the cam slot to rotate the bolt.

The charging handle is beneath the rail, in the forearm, and the handle of the charging handle portion of it can be swapped from one side to another. The charging handle reciprocates with the bolt carrier, something that was not a problem when being developed but since has caused some complaints, especially if you grab the forearm and have your hand (or more likely, your thumb) in the path of the charging handle. The first

shot causes pain. The second one doesn't, as you will have moved your hand by then. This is one aspect of having direct and close input from the end users; they sometimes want the sun, the moon and the stars, and have no idea how it should be done.

Another aspect of it came in the safety/selector. FNH-USA worked hard to get the safety just the way the guys in the dust wanted it. Then, they found that the guys didn't want it. (I'm not picking on the SO-COM dudes, they are picked for being most excellent trigger-pullers, not design or production engineers.) It

seems that a fully ambidextrous, full-sized safety paddle wasn't the perfect design. FNH-USA had to adjust the size of the safety and provide retrofit parts so the rifles could be used as intended. In the scheme of things, it's a minor problem.

The real trick is where the choices FNH had to make came into play. If you swap out the lower from the SCAR-L, and replace it with the lower for the SCAR-H (the 7.62 version) and swap bolts and barrels, you have the same rifle in 7.62. With 80% commonality, making parts becomes easier. And, since the lowers are not serial-numbered, they are not controlled parts. If someone wants to buy a SCAR, then buy the conversion parts (once FNH-USA gets up to speed on it) he could have two rifles in one.

The 7.62 version uses its own magazines, derivatives of the FAL metric magazines, but making those is not difficult. And, depending on just how different they are, you might even be able to take dirt-cheap metric FAL mags and modify them to fit in your SCAR-H.

At the National Guard base, hosing down 300-meter targets. Even with iron sights, a piece of cake.

The SCAR works with bullets of any weight.

The big boomer of the FNH-USA stable, the 40mm grenade launcher.

I've shot the SCAR in several versions, and once I had a chance to handle them, I had a few ideas of how things would pan out. Recent buzz from the Mountain Resort have indicated that I may be middle-aged, with bad knees, but I still can figure a few things; it seems the Special forces, and SOCOM folks who have been trying it, prefer the 7.62 SCAR-H.

Look at it from the perspective of a design engineer: you have been given the assignment to make a rifle that can be swapped back and forth from 5.56 to 7.62. You have three choices: you make a 7.62-weight rifle, which would result in a really fat 5.56. The M4, loaded with gear, can be nearly 10 pounds. No one wants a new 5.56 that starts out at 10 pounds before gear, no matter how much better it may be. OK, so you go the other way; you make a new 5.56 that weighs under six pounds. The original AR-15 did that. I've built an XM-177A2 clone that tips the scales at just over 5.5 pounds. But do that and your 7.62 version won't be strong enough to last. It will break under hard use or heavy firing schedules.

FNH-USA has their own 3-gun competition team, and they use SCARs with little or no mods. Here, the only change is to a comp this particular shooter prefers.

The FNH-USA IAR for the army trials.

A rifle? No. tactical? Very. Fun? You have to ask? An FNH-USA built M240B.

The FNH-USA IAR changes to an open-bolt mode of operation when the internal temperature gets high enough.

Yes, lots of fun. And surprisingly stout recoil. Of course, at less than seven pounds, you'd expect that.

Which, by the way, was the fate of one of the SPIW candidates back in the earliest days. The weight limit was unrealistically low. Three candidates were over the weight limit. The fourth one was under the limit, but the test panel deemed it unsafe to even test, it was so lightly built.

So you go ahead and split the difference but shade your design to be as light as you can, while still being durable. You end up with a rifle that in 5.56 is 6.7 pounds and in 7.62 is 7.8 pounds. And to no one's surprise, given the choice, the guys who actually shoot people for a living would rather have a 7.8-pound 7.62 than a 6.7-pound 5.56.

Remember, up to this point, your typical 7.62 NATO rifle would be lucky to even get close to 8.5 pounds. Most run over nine pounds. Again, this is before bolting on optics, lasers, lights, etc. So an under-eight pound 7.62, with quick-change barrels (the guys who shoot people do a lot of shooting, and don't have time to wait around for a brigade-level armorer to swap out worn barrels) easy-mount scopes, and piston reliability is a beautiful thing.

And, being a piston design, it is ready to go to mount a suppressor on, something the direct-gas systems can have problems with. The government, via SOCOM, has recently stopped acquisition of the Mk 16 (the 5.56 model) and shifted the funding to the Mk 17 (the 7.62 version) due to the requests of the end users who want more big-bore rifles.

The FNH-USA grenade launcher is a single-shot.

The SCAR: heavy, accurate, soft in recoil, fun to shoot, and soon available.

Not to be left out of any opportunity to get a foot in, FNH-USA also makes versions that we may never see but are being shown to the military

The Precision Rifle is a purpose-built semi-auto sniper rifle, with all attention turned to making it accurate while not decreasing its reliability. Also known as the Mk20 Sniper Support (and what sniper wants to be "supported" by a Mk20, when he could be using it instead of a bolt gun?) I had a chance to shoot this one, also, and it sports a muzzle brake made by PWS that will also accept a suppressor. In many instances, the designs of muzzle brakes have not been undertaken with the idea of putting a suppressor on. And the future of the military is for greater and greater suppressor use. The PWS brake is so effective that when I was taking photos of it, standing in the best spot for the photo (which Murphy's Law, being what it is, placed well within the blast cone of the brake), I thought I was going to lose my hat or earmuffs. Once I had a chance behind the rifle, there was no head-sized rock within the limits of the range (there was a ridge running some 600 yards out, and we could not shoot above the ridge-line) that was safe. And best of all, since the Precision Rifle is based on the SCAR, any armorer who knows

how to work on a SCAR can keep a Precision Rifle working. Also, if someone needs to "pinch-hit" on the Precision Rifle, everything is the same except for the level of accuracy – which is nothing to sneeze about on the SCAR, by the way.

As if that weren't enough, FNH-USA also developed a light machine gun on the SCAR. The Individual Automatic Rifle is essentially a 5.56 BAR. The trick thing here is the trigger mechanism. When on semi, it fires from a closed bolt, for best accuracy. On full, or when it heats up, it switches to open-bolt operation, for greater cooling. Now, the idea to replace the SAW with a box magazine-fed one is not new. And for squad-level use, the idea has a lot of merit. Typically (or so I've been told) at the squad level, the ammo capacity that a belt-fed offers isn't all that useful. It isn't like you're going to use a SAW for fire suppression or area denial, it hasn't the range. And belts collect all kinds of debris, smut and gunk.

So, for a 5.56 BAR, the IAR has a lot going for it. However, if you're armed with 7.62 SCARs, a 5.56 full-auto support weapon doesn't make a lot of sense. And let us be absolutely clear on this point: trying to take a 5.56 IAR and convert it to 7.62, or convert a 7.62

SCAR into an IAR is a very bad idea. That was one of the things that caused the M14 to be dropped and left by the wayside – it was too light. And it was nearly 10 pounds, not under eight. "But, but, the original BAR was a wonder-weapon." Yes, and it was 18 to 19 pounds, almost three times the weight of a SCAR-H. The FNH-USA IAR was not selected by the USMC, who elected to go with the HK 416 variant instead. Which makes sense in the convoluted, bizarre world of military procurement. Rather than have a new (and arguably better) automatic rifle, with a different manual of arms, controls, nomenclature, etc., why not adopt one that is as closer to the existing rifle as possible? Sigh.

Now, just to add a cap to the SCAR, the modern military unit is not complete without some sort of grenade-throwing device. No, not a strong right arm, but an M406, H-E grenade, fired from some sort of shoulder-mount or weapon-mount barrel. The originals were the XM-148 of Vietnam, but the M-203 was quickly adopted. And there it remains. Despite advances in design and fuses, the armed forces still use a single-shot grenade launcher. Again, sigh.

However, FNH-USA has come up with another advance. Not necessarily their own bright idea, but the new grenade launcher hinges open to the side. That means you can have a short, compact weapon, and still stuff the overly-long parachute flare and other rounds into it. The FN40GL, aka the Mk 13 Mod 0. is a cute little beast, if a device that can hurl high explosives hundreds of meters downrange can be called cute.

It fits underneath the forearm of the SCAR, and it adds a long-range punch to the squad or platoon that can be most welcome. It is plenty accurate, as most of the Mk406-launching devices are, but due to the really looping trajectory, knowing the range is important. If you know the range, and can account for the wind, you can throw a grenade through a window at several hundred meters. I had an afternoon to play with one, and I was surprised at how much even a light wind could blow the grenades.

Maybe we'll see an all-SCAR Army in the future. Then again, if we go by their track record, the Army, Marines, Air Force, Navy and Coasties will be using some variant (with minor upgrades) of the M16/M4 for decades to come.

Sigh.

The SCAR Precision Sniper variant, which we used to make gravel at absurd distances.

The rifled bore means the 40mm launcher is accurate, as long as you correctly divine wind drift.

# The FAL

t's late 1945. WWII has ended, and in its course, many lessons are learned. Unfortunately, the learning is not evenly distributed amongst those who will be planning for the future. The Soviets want a rifle that is essentially a glorified and gussied-up SMG. They get it, in the form of the AK-47. The British want something that is handier than the SMLE and wander down the bullpup path. Still, they have learned a few valuable lessons, perhaps most notably that a 1,000-yard match rifle is not usually needed.

Unfortunately, the US Army does not get that memo. They remain wedded to the performance of the .30-06, and use advances in powder technology to make a shorter .30-06: the .308, aka 7.62 NATO, aka T65. And they want a rifle to shoot it that does it all; the M14 (which we've looked at) was to replace the BAR, M1 Garand, M1 Carbine and the M3 SMG. Some starry-eyed dreamers think it could even replace the 1911A1, and thus make inventory and supply a simple affair. You have to wonder what was in the water.

The heart of the FAL started life as the SAFN 49. That rifle is a box-fed 7mm, 8mm or .30-06 (they made versions in each) that is charged with stripper clips. The bolt tilts down to lock, and the bottom rear catches on the locking shoulder to close the action. The shell around the bolt moves it back and forth, and tilts it up and down as needed. The magazine comes out only for cleaning, and you load by locking the bolt back and using five-round stripper clips to stuff it full. Which takes only a pair, as the magazine holds 10 rounds. A later, local-arsenal modification was to retrofit the SAFN 49 in .30-06 to accept BAR magazines, but they too were locked in, and not quickly exchanged.

The SAFN 49 has a short production and service life. It was a full-power, semi-automatic only rifle, at a time when everyone wanted to go select-fire, and many wanted to go medium-power.

Originally FN wanted to make their new post-war rifle in medium-bore cartridges. The prototypes ran on the German WWII round, the 7.92X33. Why not, there was a lot of it lying around, pretty much for the cost of collecting and shipping it. But, the US Army wanted, nay, insisted on, the .308, called the 7.62X51, and so the FAL, if it was to survive, had to be beefed up and rebuilt to take it. And so they did.

The result was a rifle that most of the free world adopted. We, however, having insisted on the .308, also insisted on the rifle we had built around it, the M14.

The FAL was adopted by more than 90 countries and purchased by some that didn't officially adopt it. Cuba, for instance, purchased a bunch of FAL rifles just before *la revolucion*, and I'd wager that they are still there, not having been fired in decades, and with the same springs still installed. The basic design is incredibly durable, but it is not without some drawbacks. But before I start dissing the FAL, let's take a look.

The rifle is your basic self-loading layout, with stock in back, receiver in the middle, complete with magazine, and handguards around the barrel up front. The action hinges open, so you can pull the bolt out and the top cover off. Unlike the AR, the upper and lower parts that hinge are not meant to be quickly dismounted. To take them apart you have to unscrew the big-head bolt (the slot is a clue) and then pinch the clothespin-like head to get them apart. Then you can separate them. The upper is the receiver (and the serial-numbered part) and from it you extract the bolt and carrier. The carrier has a long rod attached that presses on the recoil spring that travels down into the stock.

The carrier is a shell that covers the bolt, which is a strangely-sculpted bar that gets tipped up and down by the cam slots on the inside of the carrier. Press the whole thing forward and the bolt tips down in back. Pull it back and the bolt gets lifted and then pulled back as well. The bolt tips down into a recess that has a small shoulder at the rear. The locking shoulder or shelf is a part that gets pressed into the receiver during manufacture. The barrel is screwed into the front of the receiver, and it has a washer, a spacing plate, that controls barrel lock-up.

You see, the whole rifle was designed with the idea of continual rebuilds, overhauls, updates and maintenance in mind. It was meant to last nearly forever. If, for instance, a bolt gets damaged from an excessively-loaded round, you can adjust headspace by pressing out the locking shoulder and replacing it. Armorer's kits have a precisely-ground bar with graduations on it. The armorer, when rebuilding (or building) a rifle, inserts

The Para FAL is lighter and more compact than the original design.

The DSA rear sight is very much like, and uses parts from, the AR-15 rear sight. Not only is it more durable and better protected, it is a better sight, too.

With a new barrel (or one modified by DSA) you aren't stuck with the original FAL flash hider, you can use something a lot better like this Vortex.

The recoil on an FAL is nothing to worry over. And with the adjustable gas system, you can be sure it will work with any surplus ammo you come across.

Since they make their own, DSA has all the receivers they need to ensure that your FAL is properly built.

FALs from the various countries of origin will have minor detail differences on things like sights and gas regulator. But they work the same.

the gauge, then attempts to thumb-press the bolt home. Once he knows the exact size he needs, he installs the appropriate shoulder.

Ditto with barrels, using washers of different thicknesses to adjust barrel lockup and location.

The FAL, being built by Fabrique Nationale, was made to metric dimensions. When it was adopted by the British, they could not do something so rational as simply adopt a metric-dimensioned rifle, so they had to translate everything to English measurements and compile entirely new drawings, dimensional tolerances, etc. One of the things the British changed were the magazines. Not the feed lips and such (oh, dear god, that would have been bad indeed) but the locking lugs on the magazines. So, if you are buying an FAL, or thinking of buying one, you want to know if it is metric or inch. Not that the dimensions themselves are different (barring tolerance wanderings) but things such as screw thread pitch and size differ.

The British also made a change: they did not produce theirs in select-fire, only in semi-automatic, which led, three decades later, to an odd situation during the Falklands War, where the British and Argentine forces

The lower on the FAL is not the receiver, unlike the AR-15. It is just a thing that holds essential parts.

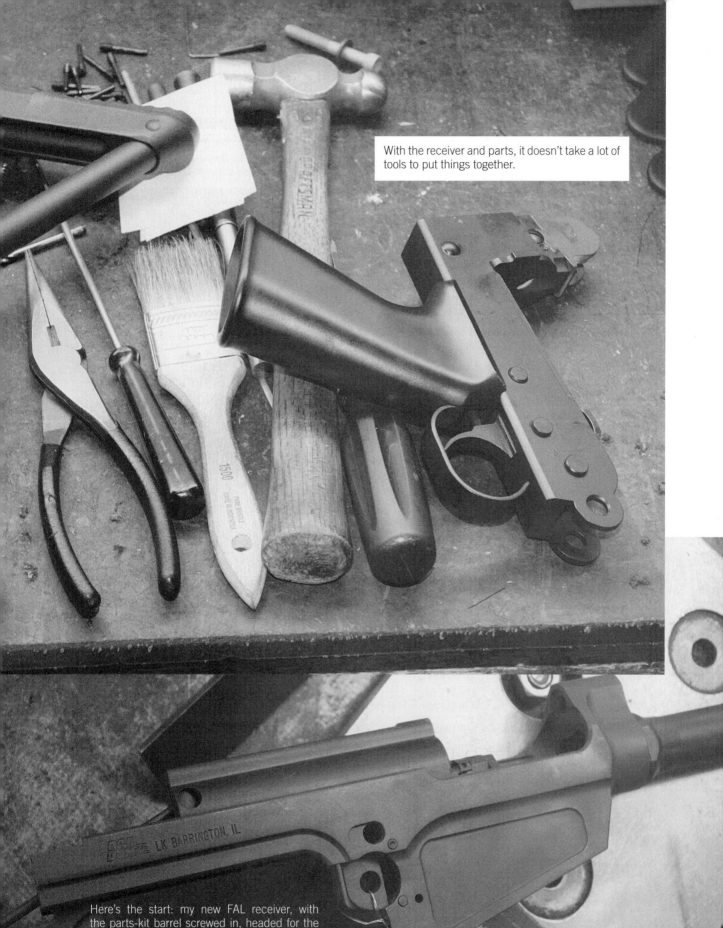

With the receiver and parts, it doesn't take a lot of tools to put things together.

Here's the start: my new FAL receiver, with the parts-kit barrel screwed in, headed for the headspace test it will fail. (The barrel's fault, not the receiver's.)

were not only using the same rifles (inch on the British side and metric on the Argy) in their FALs, but also in their P-35 pistols.

Today, the biggest producer of FAL rifles is DSA, in Illinois. I went there with my Indian (inch-pattern) FAL parts kit, to have them build me a Para FAL, pretty much along the pattern of the 50.63 Model. Things were not good from the start.

A small bit of backstory on my parts kit: when it came time to adopt the FAL, India asked FN for prototypes they could test. FN duly shipped a selection of rifles. India tested them and found they liked them. So India, instead of negotiating for a license to manufacture (or so the story goes, which I believe) India simply handed FN a check for the invoiced amount of the test rifles. FN had the last laugh, as the rifles were an amalgam of hand-built models, some say deliberately out-of-spec. India, in trying to reverse-engineer the rifles to make their own, had no idea of which dimension was correct. They settled on what worked and made rifles. But since their parts were not interchangeable with other license-built rifles, they could not go out and market their rifles. Who'd buy them, knowing

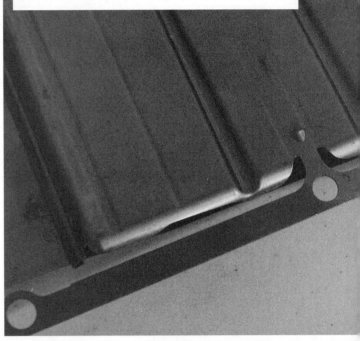

DSA is making their own magazines now. (As well they can; they bought the forming dies from the Austrians). This is an early step in the process.

The front sight/gas block has the op rod guide tube silver-soldered to it. Then, the assembly is press-fit to the barrel.

My Para FAL is not any longer than an AR-15 carbine but hits a lot harder.

The DSA lower is made from aluminum, which takes weight off the rifle and is still plenty durable.

The Para FAL is no longer than, no heavier than, and less costly than, the current crop of high-end AR-15s. No scope, you say? DSA can solve that quickly, with just a new receiver cover.

DSA does custom work and has moved beyond the original models that FN created. You want a folding stock SBR FAL? No problem, once you get the paperwork sorted out.

round inside, with the thickest locking shelf available. Sigh. Off came the kit barrel, and a new barrel (inch pattern) came off the shelf to be fitted. It went on without a problem.

And so on with the rest of the parts. By the time I was done, almost all the original Indian parts kits parts were back in the cardboard box they had traveled to DSA in, and the few Indian parts that made the grade were in my rifle. At that point it was too late, but had I known how things would go I probably would have elected to go with an all-metric build, as magazines are far more common in metric than inch pattern.

Then we test-fired. Oh, frak, it didn't cycle. More measuring and checking, and more parts swapping, and it finally ran through a magazine, no problem. I have to point out again that the headaches we encountered were due to my parts kit. If you have a metric, or British-made, inch-pattern parts kit, you'll be fine. But if yours is an Indian kit, be prepared to get your rifle back after it went through much the same process mine did – and with a resulting invoice to boot. It really isn't worth it to buy an Indian parts kit, so don't.

DSA is making new magazines, along with other parts. You see, they bought the entire Austrian FAL manufacturing factory, when Austria decided they really didn't need it in reserve after all. Tons and tons of parts, tooling, gauges, etc, came to Illinois, and were promptly stuffed it into a DSA warehouse.

All that tooling, and those parts, allowed DSA the freedom to build what they want, which is how they came to build FAL sniper variants when the Army opened up requests for a semi-automatic sniper system. As explained to me by Mark Christiansen, the marketing guru at DSA: "We knew the Army wouldn't pick an FAL-based system, they wanted something that was 'more modern' and hi-tech. But we wanted to demonstrate that we could run with anyone, and we did." I got to handle the test rifles, complete with free-float forearms, adjustable cheekpieces, and scope mounts. Looking at them, I couldn't help but wonder how things could have gone, had we adopted the FAL in 1957 instead of the M14.

My Para FAL, my metric/inch frankengun, tips the scales at just over eight pounds, due in part to the aluminum lower receiver. That is one of the things that DSA was able to do, since they had the gauges. They make lowers from aluminum instead of steel, which takes a lot of weight off. At 16 inches, my barrel also removes some weight.

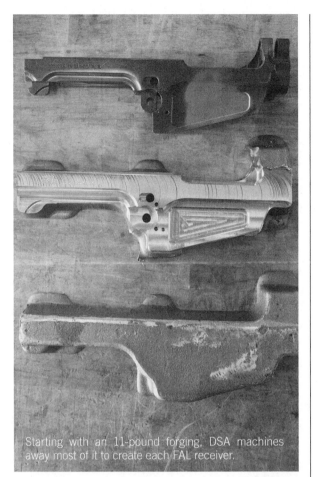

Starting with an 11-pound forging, DSA machines away most of it to create each FAL receiver.

that India and India alone could supply spares? My parts kit was purchased some 20 years ago, before parts kits were common, and before we knew as much about the FAL as we do now.

Fast-forward to the present day. I showed up at DSA with my parts kit in hand, and the fun began. (Oh, I should point out right now that you should not arrive with your parts kit. If you want one built, DSA will be happy to receive the package via UPS/FedEx. But not personally.) "Oh, this part won't do. This is out of spec. This is busted." And so on. By the time we had pored through the parts, I was not going to have any problem meeting the 922(r) compliance requirements. Then we started assembling.

First up, the barrel. The armorer screwed it on, and it screwed right past the witness mark. So, out came the thickest barrel washer in the building, and we tried again. OK, now it was too thick, so we used a surface grinder to gradually thin it until the barrel locked up correctly. In went the headspace gauge, and in went the headspace bolt rod. The chamber was over-long, so much so that we could hear the headspace gauge rattle

We had to surface-grind a new barrel washer in the vain attempt at making my parts kit barrel work.

Here you see the locking shoulder gauge. Once the assembler has measured which shoulder is needed, he simply presses that one in place.

The various arsenals that made the FAL also made cut-away versions for armorer's instruction.

Here is the locking shoulder being pressed into place.

Shorty? No problem.

Gew.Kal.7.62mm.F.N.

This is notable not only for being a factory cut-away, but also for being marked as the German FAL, which they called the G1.

The original was so long, it isn't even all in this photo.

I'm 6'4" tall, and the standard FAL (inch or metric) runs 43 inches. In any kind of low ready position, the flash hider is down past my knees. I can't see how someone shorter than 5'10" can expect to use it and keep the muzzle out of the grass and mud.

The new DSA upper uses an AR-like rear sight, with easy adjustments and protective sight wings, instead of the folding "popsicle stick" rear sight. Coming from an L1A1-like parts kit, my carrier is angle-cut to chop sand and debris, and the charging handle folds on the left side.

The stock folds, which makes it compact, but brings another problem; a short length of pull. Standing, I have no problem, but if I go prone, the rear of the receiver bumps my nose when firing. I'm going to have to either wear some sort of vest or carrier, to add thickness, or wrap the buttplate with paracord to add just a bit more pull.

And, since it is based on an inch-pattern receiver, I have to use inch-pattern magazines. Some will tell you that inch-pattern rifles use metric mags, but my experience has been: not so much. You might bet lucky, but mostly you'll be disappointed.

I took my Para FAL to a patrol rifle class and shot a passing qual score with it, to no one's surprise. One

The FAL mags, on the left the inch-pattern, and on the right the metric. Metrics are supposed to work in inch guns, but often don't. Inch mags won't fit at all into a metric rifle.

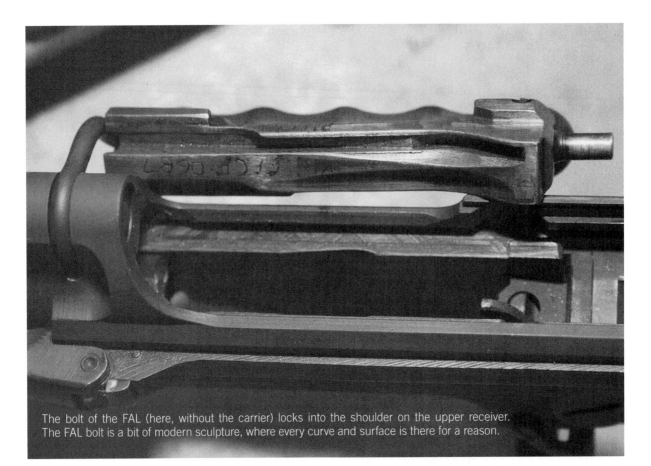

The bolt of the FAL (here, without the carrier) locks into the shoulder on the upper receiver. The FAL bolt is a bit of modern sculpture, where every curve and surface is there for a reason.

of the instructors that day was Henk Iverson, who has had much experience in South Africa with the FAL. He remarked that when they went with the R4, the SA-made Galil, the police quickly found that it could not get into vehicles. They promptly went back to the armory, turned in their R4s, and checked out R1s, the South African-built FALS, in many instances the very ones they had been using before. Those were full-sized, and Henk allowed as how my Para would have been very handy.

You may ask, "If most FALs were made as select-fire, what happens when I build one?" Simple: the critical part is the upper, which is the firearm. And as a parts kit, that is the part that is destroyed by regulation. The upper has an access slot for the linkage to connect the selector, when set on "Auto" to the carrier, to trip the sear. Your semi-auto only new upper won't have any place for the linkage to connect, and thus will be kosher, at least in that regard. You'll still have to make sure it is 922(r) compliant.

There is one rifle out there that has the slot, is lawful, and yet is not a machine gun. Back when Browning was first importing the FAL, they got approval to bring in a bunch of FALs with the upper receiver slot, but with semi-auto only parts installed. After they had been brought in, it was discovered that they were, in effect, machineguns in waiting. Now, since this happened back when those involved were still rational, a simple solution was found: those rifles were permitted to be owned, and exist as semi-auto rifles, by serial number. If you have one, it is a fabulously expensive collector's item. And you must not, under any circumstances, own it along with a fistful of conversion parts. That would be a no-no. For the rest of us, the FAL is the semi-auto right arm of the free world.

One big deal about the FAL system is the gas system. It is a piston, with a connecting rod between the valve and the carrier, with a return spring for the connecting rod. The valve is adjustable. The adjustment process is simple: turn the valve to the lowest setting, the one that feeds the least gas to the rifle. Load a magazine with a single round. Fire it. The bolt won't lock open. Click the setting to one higher, and repeat. Do this until the rifle locks open consistently, and then give the gas setting one more click toward "more gas." You're set.

Now get out there and shoot.

# PDWs

As tactical rifles go, the PDW, or Personal Defense Weapon, is not exactly tacti-cool. Well, it is, for it is compact, desired, and in some models unobtainable. But as a tool to get your neck out of a hot spot, it is not what I'd grab first.

What exactly is a PDW? Well, according to NATO, it is a compact, select-fire weapon of less than rifle caliber, capable of penetrating body armor at more than muzzle-blast distances. Except for the excessive body armor/helmet requirement, we've had PDWs for a long time, starting with the stocked, select-fire Mauser and Spanish copies of the Mauser C96 broomhandle of 1896. A whole raft of compact submachine guns could be considered as PDWs, if they only would penetrate armor well enough. (They can, but that is for a bit later.)

The intent of the PDW is to provide the not-front-line combatants with a reasonably serious fighting tool, but one that will be less bulky and ponderous than an issue rifle. By that, they are thinking of truck driver, radio operators (not those in the field with a maneuvering unit, however), mortar and artillery units, etc. The idea is that they will be able to put up a good fight with a weapon capable of doing the job out to 150 meters or so.

The first real entrant that might be considered a PDW was the M1 Carbine. It fired the .30 Carbine cartridge, which was a 110-grain FMJ of .308" diameter, at something on the order of 1900 fps. The M1 Carbine is a subject of some controversy. While it was used by many in WWII in both the European and Pacific theaters, it failed in Korea. Some attribute it to the quilted clothing worn by Chinese soldiers in the bitter cold of a Korean winter; some, to re-built weapons not having been properly re-built or maintained; and others, to the much greater use of the M2 variant, the select-fire one, and basically a failure of timing. That is, if GIs used the M2 in semi- or full-auto fire from the beginning of an engagement, it would be overheated and nearly out of ammo by the time you really needed it, with Chicom soldiers pouring over the wire. Still others derided it for its lack of power.

Which I find curious, as I've mentioned before. The late Jim Cirillo, famed of the NYPD Stakeout Squad, reported that the M1 carbine (and with a shortened barrel, no less) was the only firearm he or anyone else used that had an absolute 100% record of DRT. Dead Right There.

What fascinates me is the insistence on penetrating body armor, despite body armor evolving so quickly that it will stop (in some models) full-powered rifle ammo. So, you're going to make something not a whole lot bigger than a 1911, and actually no bigger than an UZI, and with it you're going to shoot through armor that can stop .30-06 AP? Get real. To make matters even siller, the prospect of an opponent wearing body armor, while possible, is of such a low likelihood as to be non-existent.

So, let's abandon the idea of an armor-piercing round, since it is an idiotic requirement anyway. (And you can quote me at the next meeting of NATO ex-

The lineup of the possible: .45, 9mm 5.7 and 5.56

The idea of a PDW is simple: a just larger-than-handgun-sized firearm, that does a lot more, almost as much as a rifle. Too bad there's no such thing as a free lunch.

One of the original PDWs, the M3 "Grease Gun." A .45 ACP SMG, it was meant for close-range defense.

Handgun cartridges lack range (not usually a problem for close-distance defense) and penetration for PDW use.

perts who are trying to find a PDW to adopt.) What we are left with is a compact, accurate and easy to shoot firearm that will deliver at least an incapacitating blow, if not a fully-powerful one by rifle standards. That includes a lot of new PDW cartridges (probably all of them) and more than a few handgun cartridges.

Wait a minute, you say. Back up. Why aren't handguns considered PDWs? Well, they are to those who actually practice and expect to use firearms. The big problem the insider experts have with handguns is not that they lack range, which I'll readily admit. While my friends and I have a great deal of fun trying our skills on the US Army combat rifle course with our handguns, we are under no illusions that it is anything more than a stunt and a fun time. While we routinely drop the targets out to 150 meters, we aren't being shot at. And without the decades of practice we've had, most people have a tough time dropping the 50 meter tar-

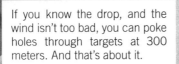

If you know the drop, and the wind isn't too bad, you can poke holes through targets at 300 meters. And that's about it.

gets, let alone have a chance at the 100 meter ones.

Which misses the whole point of a handgun: you have it because it is handy, not because it is the hammer of Thor. It is a 25-yards-and-closer weapon, and it being issued to the troops should be a case of "in addition to" and not "instead of" a main weapon or a PDW.

There is, besides the M1 Carbine, another possibility for the PDW: the SMG. Submachineguns have been used in various armed forces since their development

Some advocate short-barreled rifles as PDWs. The trouble is, they are impressively loud, have huge flash, and often are mechanically unreliable. Fun, though.

The Soviet PDW, the mis-named Krinkov, is common in some overseas locales.

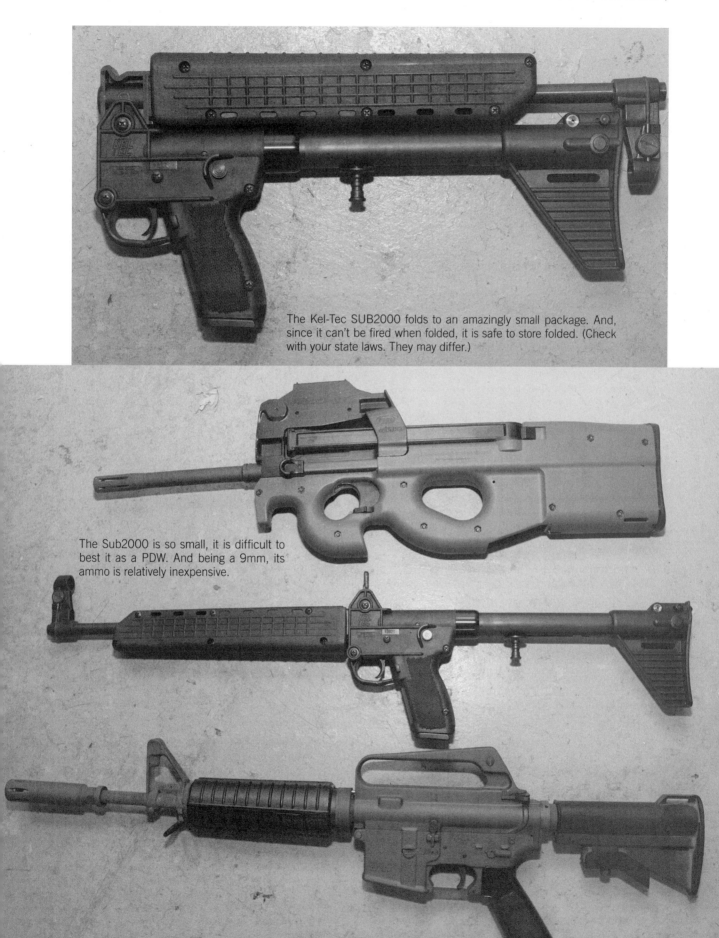

The Kel-Tec SUB2000 folds to an amazingly small package. And, since it can't be fired when folded, it is safe to store folded. (Check with your state laws. They may differ.)

The Sub2000 is so small, it is difficult to best it as a PDW. And being a 9mm, its ammo is relatively inexpensive.

Properly made, they lack nothing in accuracy. Here is a 1X-down qualification score.

The PDW, here as the PS90, does what it can in ballistic gelatin.

in WWI. They were at their peak between WWI and WWII, and used extensively during the latter. However, they fell out of favor for several reasons. One had to do with the very attractiveness of the SMG; low production cost. While you could easily stamp and machine the parts to make a STEN, a PPS-43 or an M3, what you ended up with was just that: a stamped SMG with casual accuracy at best. While there was a war on, any gun was good, and something cheap and durable very good. But, given a choice, even end-users wanted something a little more refined, a little more accurate, or a little more powerful.

If you machine an SMG from forgings or billet, well, you've now invested the same amount of time, effort and cost into a somewhat more accurate SMG that you would have in a much more accurate and powerful rifle.

Not that an SMG won't do what the PDW devout wish for: penetration. All you have to do is make your 9mm ammo with a steel core, or a copper-clad steel jacket, at full velocity or perhaps a bit more, and it will penetrate all but rifle-rated body armor.

The trick designers of PDWs have is this: those desiring a PDW for the troops are asking the sun, the moon and the stars. They want a weapon that delivers much of the power of a carbine (such as an M4) or a full-sized rifle (the M16 or AK series) while not having commensurate size or weight. Since weapons designers have been spending decades refining the modern small arm, reducing weight as much as they can while retaining durability and reliability, reducing size, and making them ever more capable, it is asking a lot to say, "Make me something half the size that does three-quarters of the job."

One of the problems of very compact weapons is in trying to wrap yourself around them to use them.

A PDW is so handy (here, as an SBR) that even though meant for "just" defense, it will end up in the hands of front-line troops, just as the M1 Carbine did.

Regardless of how handy, it still has to be useful. The MP7 is very useful, but not overly powerful. Oh well.

Basically, you're asking them to make a Ford Ranger or a Chevy S-10 do most of the work of a Humvee, but without the weight. Good luck with that.

That does not keep people from trying. The old-school (at least, "old-school" now that we're in the 21st century) PDW would be an HK MP5K with a folding stock (not the miserable telescoping stock of the original MP5 design). It is accurate, reliable, and holds enough ammo. Next up is the FN P90. Those who have watched the TV series "Stargate" will be quite familiar with it, even if they haven't seen it in person or fired it. The select-fire version has a 10-inch barrel while the semi-only version has a 16-inch barrel. It is a bullpup PDW, and the magazine is also unique in that it lies parallel to the barrel, and rotates each round down in turn.

A compact firearm, here the HK MP7, can be very handy.

The ballistics of the HK 4.6 round are not going to amaze you.

As compact as the 5.7 and other PDW ammo is, you can fit a lot in magazines, and shipping it doesn't take a lot of room. A standard ammo can holds 2,000 rounds.

The second HK entrant is the P7, more of a hand-gun-with-a-stock-and-a-small-rifle-round design than anything else. The magazine well is the pistol grip, in much the same way as the Uzi design uses the pistol grip as the magazine well.

Finally, we have the Knight's Armament KAC-PDW using the AR design as a template but with much different internals. The result is a compact firearm that allows for a folding stock, something not possible on your typical AR. (The cognoscenti will immediately remember the Para Tactical Target rifle.) Now the Knight's PDW is very interesting. But we need not go that far to get ourselves to an AR-based PDW.

I recently built a Retro AR, a copy of the XM-177.

Retro fans will know it as the Colt 610. With a 16-inch barrel and faux suppressor, it tips the scales at 5.66 pounds. If we take my Retro, and install a Para-type gas and recoil system on it, so we can install a folding stock, we have a very compact carbine. If we then trim the barrel to 11.5 inches, and install a short suppressor so we don't blow our own ears off, we can have a compact carbine that comes very close to the Knight's PDW, or even the P90, in weight and size. It also does not require a different ammunition and magazines in the supply system, and does not require any different training than that of your standard M16/M4.

But hey, the NATO experts who lust after a PDW don't ask my opinion. So, let's look over what we can of the PDW-verse, and see what we come up with, eh?

## PS90

While it is common to refer to both versions as the P90, to be correct you have to keep in mind that there are two versions, and that you will likely only ever see one of them, the semi-auto version. Why? FOPA '86.

The HK 4.6 is also a diminutive round, shown here next to a 5.56, it makes the 5.56 look like a magnum.

The selector on the MP7 shows its intent: safe, semi and "Repel All Boarders."

A 20-round magazine for the MP7 is so compact, it fits in the hand.

The Firearms Owners Protection Act of 1986 had a small amendment added at the last minute (literally): one that prohibited the new manufacture of machine-guns.

So the only select-fire P90s you will see will be in the hands of your local police department or sheriff's office. Now, you may see some short-barreled ones. That is relatively easy. You see, while you can't have a newly-made machine gun, you can have (in the states that allow it) a firearm be turned into an SBR, a short-barreled rifle, which is wicked cool.

The PS90, the semi-auto only version, is the same firearm as the P90, but with a short barrel and the necessary (and fun) select-fire parts inside removed.

The '90 is built around the 5.7 cartridge – to be exact, the 5.7X28. The 5.7 began as the SS90, a specialized round using a 23-grain bullet at some 2800 fps. However, as you'd expect, the downrange oomph of such a combo is somewhat limited. So, the bullet weight has gone up, and the velocity down, since then. We now have a number of variants of the loading, from the SS190, a design using a steel penetrator and an aluminum core, which is not for sale outside of law enforcement here in the U.S. Not because of FN policies but because the same ammo also fits in the FN FiveseveN pistol, and thus the SS190 is "armor-piercing handgun ammunition," which is prohibited for sale by Federal law.

No problem, as there is a lot of other ammo for sale, ammo that doesn't meet the definition of AP under Federal regs but works just fine, defensively.

That ammunition feeds out of the unique magazine of the P/PS90, a horizontally-mounted device in which the rounds are positioned transversely to the axis of the bore. The magazine design is patented (US patent 4,905,394) and as far as I know FN has not licensed the design to anyone else.

The PS90 (what we're going to look at, since we can't get the select-fire version, neither you, the reader, nor I) is a bullpup, blowback design with an ambidextrous grip shape and safety design, and bottom-ejection.

To load and fire, you simply stuff the box end of the magazine (loaded, of course) forward under the front sight housing tower. Then snap the rounded end of the magazine down into place (raised section down) into the receiver, and latch it under the latch. The spring-loaded latch will move out of the way as you press the magazine down, and snap back to hold it in place. Grab the charging handle, pull back and let go. Turn the safety to "1" and press the trigger. There will be a semi-loud noise, a bullet out the front, and a hole in your target. The empty case falls out the bottom.

The magazine is a thing of beauty and simplicity. The feed lips of the raised section have been machined as a spiral, and each round rotates a quarter-turn as you either press it in place to load it, or as it comes down, feeding into the receiver. No levers, springs, cams, arms, etc. to move things, just a spiral 3-D ramp.

The design is blowback, which is one small impediment to reloading. The chamber/shoulder dimensions are interesting. If you take a round and chamber it, then extract it, and compare it to an unchambered round, it seems pretty clear that the loaded cartridge/chamber fit is a crush fit, with the bolt slamming the shoulder of

Unless you have some pressing need for armor penetration, a PDW in 9mm has a lot to recommend it. Starting with the latest expanding bullet technology.

The Kel-Tec SUB2000 folds to an amazingly small package. And, since it can't be fired when folded, it is safe to store folded. (Check with your state laws. They may differ.)

the round into the chamber wall. Also, clearly, a fired case has its shoulder pushed forward, showing that it is an unlocked, blowback action. While it may be possible to improve the ballistics of the round, chambering it in a bolt-action rifle, what's the point?

The reloading impediment comes when you try to find a shell holder to hang onto the diminutive case. Then, setting the shoulder back work-hardens it, so you may not get many firings out of it before it splits. Plus there are persistent rumors that there is a wax applied to the case when made, to provide reliable function. Without that wax (if it exists) your reloads may not be as reliable as factory ammo.

The recoil is almost insubstantial. I had a chance to visit the FN plant in Liege, Belgium, in 2000. There, I fired the P90, as well as the FiveseveN handgun. With a bit of practice (less than a magazine) I found I could brace myself and keep all my shots from a burst on a target at 100 meters. Using the SB193, subsonic ammo, and a suppressor, the loudest noise was the bolt cycling back and forth, and the empties hitting the concrete.

The trigger on the P90 has the safety wheel marked "S" "1" and "A." The A setting is the auto setting, with a trigger that works in a manner like the Steyr AUG. A controlled press fires a single shot, but a quick grab on the trigger gets you a burst, until you let go. That hardest part of the exercise is learning to clutch the trigger

and still keep the sights on the target.

As a semi-auto rifle, the PS90 has some very interesting possibilities. For someone new to shooting, it provides a nearly recoil-free and low-sound shooting experience. (While comparable in noise and recoil to a .22LR, the ammo cost of the 5.7X8 is perhaps 10 times greater.) If you wanted to teach someone who was new to firearms, the use of a defensive rifle, this would be it. The controls are simple, the recoil nothing, and the performance quite good. No, it is not a 5.56 in performance. It also is not a 5.56 in noise and recoil.

And let's be clear about this: you are basically shooting a self-loading .22 Hornet. The heavy bullets are 40 grains and exit the immediate vicinity at just under 2,000 fps. The lighter ones are just over it. This is not 5.56 territory, nor even close to it. A short-barreled AR-15 or M16, SBR'd to 10.5 inches, is going to hurl a 55-grain FMJ at well over 2300 fps, maybe more depending on the particular load. Bump that up to 11.5 for reliable function, and the velocity becomes over 2400 fps, so you have a 20% increase in velocity and a 37.5% increase in weight. You do get a horrific amount of muzzle blast too, but that's the price you pay.

Could FN have made the P90 and the PS90 more? Sure. But, the cost would have been too much. To boost the weight of the 5.7 bullet a bit, and the velocity probably would have meant they could not go with

The Kel-Tec folds right in front of the trigger guard.

The "Sub" is so small, you could stuff it into a backpack and not have it show. That could be very handy, in a COMWEC (Complete Meltdown of Western Civilization) situation.

a blowback. A locked-breech design adds more bulk, weight and complexity. If you go much bigger, you enter the AR SBR area, and then you lose the advantage. A PDW that is no smaller, lighter or easier to use than a Colt Commando might as well be a Colt Commando.

No, the PS90 is what it is, and delivers what it delivers. If you can, and you shortened it (lawfully, please) to an SBR, it would make an even handier defensive rifle for someone who is noise and recoil-shy.

## HK

The HK entry in the PDW wars is the MP7. Unlike the P90, the MP7 is a rotating-bolt, locked-breech system. Also unlike the 5.7, the HK cartridge, the 4.6X30 uses a core that is steel, without any concession to softpoints, hollowpoints or the like. Well, that is the HK position, but not that of people who make the ammo for them. More on that in a bit.

Unlike the bullpup layout of the P90, the MP7 is

a conventional design on the exterior, with the double-stack magazine going into the receiver via the pistol grip. It takes magazines of 20, 30 and 40 rounds, the 20-round variant being flush with the pistol grip. This allows for a compact pistol/carbine/whatever that can be worn (you don't really sling something this compact, you wear it) and yet can be quickly loaded with higher-capacity magazines.

The MP7 is easy to handle, but it demonstrates an effect that the proponents of the PDW seem to have overlooked: when you make something smaller, it becomes more handy. That is, until it becomes so small that you have to slow down to use it. We've all seen this with cell phones. Once a phone, calculator, etc.

Given the minimal recoil, full-magazine dumps do not shove the shooter around at all.

becomes too small, pressing the buttons becomes difficult.

And so it can be with firearms. Once it becomes small enough, you spend more time just getting yourself wrapped around it than you would with something bigger. Now maybe this isn't the case for others, but the MP7 is enough smaller to me that I find I am slower using it than other firearms.

The ballistics are no more impressive than the 5.7. The 4.6mm bullet, .18 caliber, is zippy at 2340 fps, but that is with the 25-grain copper-plated steel core. As an armor-piercing handgun round, we aren't going to get any of that. The 40-grain FMJ or JHP is traveling at 1900 fps, the same as the 5.7. Which is no great surprise, as they are similarly-proportioned and capacity cartridges.

Unlike the PS90, there is no semi-auto only MP7. You and I won't be able to acquire one, short of the breakdown of civilization and/or the zombie apocalypse. But it sure is fun to shoot.

## Kel-Tec Sub 2000

So, what is something we can get as a PDW, with commonly-available ammo, and still compact enough to be close at hand in a COMWEC scenario? (COMWEC; the complete meltdown of western civilization.) Simple: the Kel-Tec Sub2000.

The Sub is a 9mm (and .40, for them that has to have the bigger bore) carbine that feeds from Glock magazines. Now, if you find yourself in a bad situation, and resupply is chancy or not going to happen, depending on finding 9mm ammo and Glock magazines is a pretty good bet.

The Sub2000 folds, going from 29.5 inches down to 16 inches, an attribute that causes an attack of the vapors in some folks. "Sixteen inches? That's SBR territory? How can they sell it?" Simple: the Feds measure a folding-stock rifle with the stock extended. If you want to measure it folded you can, but you can't shoot it folded. The very clever design hinges open at the breech, so when it is folded the bolt can't come anywhere near the chamber. The rear sight folds when you fold the carbine, so the package is extremely compact, and the sight adjustments are all done to the front sight. That makes the rear sight, a popsicle stick with an aperture in it, as simple as can be.

Once folded, it latches onto the sight, and the rifle stays folded. It won't flop open on you. It is a straight blowback, with the charging handle underneath the stock tube, which also contains the recoil spring. As a 9mm it has a pretty bouncy recoil, and in .40 it is somewhat harsh. But that is part of the price for such compactness, and for the light weight. How light? How about four pounds, empty?

Folded, at 16 inches, it would slip right into a backpack or book bag and pass un-noticed. If you found yourself at work in a hurricane, earthquake or some such event, you could have a folded SUB2000 in your gear, and no one would notice. (Alert! Alert! Let us be absolutely clear: I'm not advocating packing a firearm in your gear in locations, jurisdictions or in situations where it is not lawfully permitted. Consult your attorney before proceeding to rig your backpack or attaché case to hold something, anything, let alone a SUB2000.)

The Sub2000 is made mostly of polymers, but with the important parts made of steel. In talking with Kel-Tec I find they have been working while I was not looking. You now have a choice not just of the 9mm or the .40, but also you can pick which magazine you want it to work with: the Glock 17, Glock 19, Beretta M92 (important for those with access to military or leo Beretta mags) S&W M59, or Sig 226.

"That's great, Sweeney, but it isn't a PDW. NATO clearly says they wanted superior armor-piercing penetration. A 9mm won't cut it." That's right. However, you won't be in their situation. They anticipated swarms of titanium-armor clad Soviet troops hustling through the Fulda Gap. Unless you are someplace you really ought not to be, you won't have that problem. In fact, you'll probably want jacketed hollow-point ammo, and not handgun AP. For that, the Sub2000 will be just the ticket.

And for the military, it is no great secret that steel-cored 9mm ammo will go through vests. In fact, pretty much anything a rifle round will go through, a steel-core 9mm will go through. And if a rifle won't, then neither a 9mm nor any PDW round will, either.

There's a test that Timothy Mullins came up with, the "Sten test." Basically, if you are considering a new wunderweapon, you should compare it in performance to a $50 Sten. (That's about what they'd cost to make, in volume.) And you know what, the new breed of PDWs do not markedly beat the Sten in performance. But, if you (or Kel-Tec, if the government asked them) were to ruggedize the SUB2000, it would perform just fine, be as compact as anything, and certainly get the job done.

## Conclusion

Me, I think the whole PDW thing is a whole lot of hooey. Issue carbines, teach people how to shoot, and give everyone in a combat zone a handgun and the training to be competent with it. Stop trying to supplant training and actual skill with equipment, and face facts: it takes time, effort dedication and a certain amount of sweat equity to be good with any weapon.

The PDW is meant to be so compact, you can almost wear it instead of carrying it.

Chapter 11

**Chapter 11**

# Ammo

Ammo is not just ammo. At the most basic level we have not changed how weapons work for millennia. The wounding mechanism used by the first man to use a spear, through the Roman army up through the introduction of firearms is the same: quickly poke a hole into or through your opponent with some sort of projectile, let the red stuff leak out, and soon he's done. Today we merely hurl the projectile farther, faster and with greater rapidity than before. The names change, but not much else.

A brief look at what you may be feeding your tactical rifle:

## Handgun Calibers

For the PDW you just were reading about, we have several.

### 9mm

The 9mm Parabellum, invented in 1904 because the German Army couldn't stomach the idea of a small-caliber handgun round, has persisted ever since for a number of reason. One is that the recoil it delivers is manageable, in just about any firearm you care to chamber it in. And that just becomes easier when the firearm has a shoulder stock. The basic round is a 115- to 125-grain bullet in the vicinity of 1100 fps. More velocity means more pressure, and that leads us to the +P and +P+ loads. While there is a +P definition from SAAMI (Small Arms and Ammunitions Manufacturers Institute) there is not for +P+. There, it is a matter of negotiation between the manufacturer and the law enforcement agency buying the ammo. (The makers do not make +P+ for general consumption.)

Were I depending on a 9mm such as the SUB2000, I'd have ammo cans full of 115- to 125-grain FMJ ammo (whatever brand/load it shot best) on hand. I'd reload for practice, shooting hard-cast lead bullets, and my defensive stash would be one of two rounds: the Winchester PDX1, or the Hornady Critical Defense. Which would I pick? Whichever one my particular SUB shot best, that's which.

### 4.6X30

The HK PDW round, it is not commonly seen for a good reason: there are no semi-auto variants, and since the MP7 has a shoulder stock it must be bought as an SBR. HK is infamous for not being all that marketing/consumer demand-friendly, and so I do not expect ever to see either a semi-auto handgun or SBR version of the MP7. If you find ammo for it, you will have an expensive collector's curiosity.

### 5.7X28

The FNH round for the PS90, P90 and the FiveseveN handgun, it is commonly available and works as advertised. The common loadings you'll see are the 40-grain V-Max bullet and the lead-free version. In either

Handguns used to be PDWs, then submachineguns were. The good old .45 and 9mm had to give way to rounds like the 5.7X28, shown here next to a 5.56.

of the FN firearms you'll likely see, it works well, as much for the low recoil and capacious magazines (50 rounds in the PS90, 20 in the FiveseveN handgun) as for any ballistic magic it might have. While the 5.7 is commonly available, one aspect that perhaps keeps it from becoming more accepted is cost. It costs as much, or more, to buy a 50-round box of 5.7 as it does 9mm. However, as the price of ammo went up, the cost differential became less of an obstacle.

Here, the choice is simple: the 40-grain V-max. I'd stock up, and use it not as an all-around but as a quiet, low-recoil round. And I'd keep firmly in mind that anyone worth shooting with it was worth hosing with it.

## Small-Bore Rounds

Here we have the 5.45 and 5.56 rounds, which can be found in just about all of the tactical rifles.

### 5.45X39

When the Soviets had caught up to the point they thought they were safe, they looked around and realized that while the AK had been the world-standard infantry rifle in 1947, by the late 1960s it was not so. They wanted something better, and they wanted the new rifle to be the same leap forward that the AK had been (curiously, the US Army was feeling pretty much the same impulse at that moment). However, in addition to the insurmountable problem of physics (we then, and

Second from the left, the Soviet 5.45X39 round, a very close approximation to the 5.56 in performance.

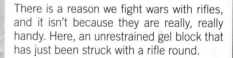

There is a reason we fight wars with rifles, and it isn't because they are really, really handy. Here, an unrestrained gel block that has just been struck with a rifle round.

The lineup of common AR rounds, next to their big brother. Left to right: 5.56, 6X45, 6.8, 6.5 and 7.62 NATO.

now, do not have any technology that can supplant our rifles with something that is 100% more effective, the desired leap) they had an additional problem: they were communists. That is, they did not have the economic base, or manufacturing wherewhithal and "headroom" to make such an investment. Not only was the problem not solvable, but they couldn't even afford to try.

So instead, they went with an improved cartridge and fiddled around the margins of the Kalashnikov.

The 5.45X39 was unveiled in the AK-74, and it got its first test in Afghanistan, when the Soviets invaded. It quickly got the nickname of the "poison bullet" rifle, due to the nasty wounds the high-velocity bullet produced. Well, that's the legend. Me, I figure that the high-velocity bullet, combined with the seventh-century level of sanitation and medical care, soon made shot people deader than Jacob Marley from infections and sepsis.

The 5.45 bullet features a steel core in a steel jacket, with a lead liner and an air tip. The alleged wounding is due to the core "moving forward on impact" and causing the bullet to tumble. Ballistic nonsense. If the core went forward, it would shift the center of mass, and make the wound track straighter, if it changed at all. No, the air pocket is probably an inadvertent detail of bullet manufacture, and fortuitously makes the bullet butt-heavy, and that is what makes it tumble on impact.

Surplus 5.45 is common, and cheap. This, of course, makes for some problems, as it was made in a number of Warsaw Pact arsenals, and quality is all over the map. And in some cases, even off the map. Bill Alexander was one of the first to offer an AR upper in 5.45, but he soon stopped. Quality was a problem. If customers buy an upper, and then buy cheap ammo which doesn't work, they are going to complain to the upper manufacturer, not the importer of the ammo.

As Bill put it once: "Imagine sitting around in an old Soviet ammo plant, during a production meeting. Someone asks 'Hey, where is that pistol powder we had?' Answer: 'We loaded it into 5.45 cases. Those Americans will pay 11 cents a round for it.'" Ouch.

Now, if that scares you, Hornady makes 5.45 here. They buy the cases, then load them with powder (and it's the correct powder) topped with a V-Max bullet. Not just good stuff, but the best.

Here, were I depending on a 5.45 (which would probably be an AK, but might be an AR) I would have to go with Soviet surplus. Not current-production, but a sealed tin or 10, dating from the Reagan era, all of the same lot, and with one can opened, tested, rifle zeroed and the remainder of the tin on stripper clips. As great as the Hornady ammo is, it isn't defensive ammo.

### .223

Here the old standby is M-193. The usual clone of it is 55-grain FMJ, loaded to relatively sedate velocities. It isn't unusual to chrono some and find that your 20-inch AR is shooting the common stuff at 2900 fps, and a carbine at less, which for most people isn't a problem. If you are plinking, or shooting in a practical match, that is all you need. And since few shoot at distance with an AR, you aren't going to notice that at 2900 fps,

The max you can get from a 5.56 round, in FMJ and for 1:12 twist barrels. This works well in all 5.56-chambered rifles.

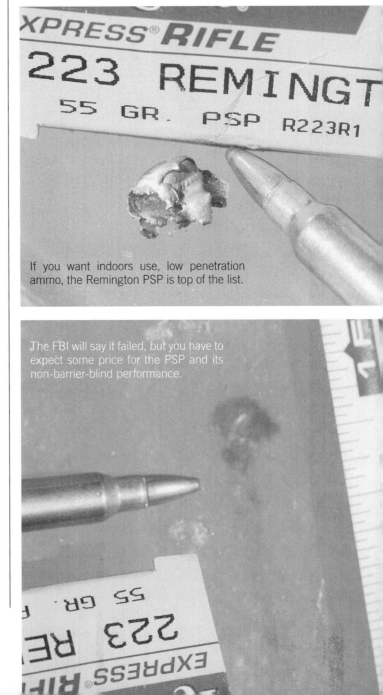

If you want indoors use, low penetration ammo, the Remington PSP is top of the list.

The FBI will say it failed, but you have to expect some price for the PSP and its non-barrier-blind performance.

Accuracy from M855 depends more on the production lot than the rifle. Here, however, the misses are the shooter's fault and not the ammo's.

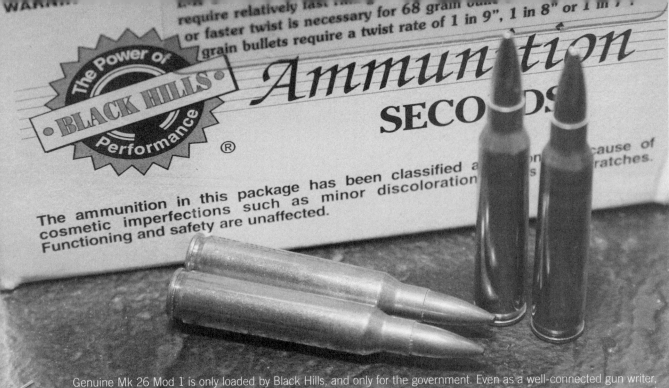

Genuine Mk 26 Mod 1 is only loaded by Black Hills, and only for the government. Even as a well-connected gun writer, I was only able to acquire a small supply of cosmetic seconds for testing. Good, the real stuff should go to the guys and gals who will use it to keep us safe.

it has a bit more drop out at 300 yards than it should otherwise have.

This isn't cheating on the part of the makers. They are doing what people want. Less noise, less muzzle blast, less wear-and-tear on rifles, everyone is happy. Except those of us who want performance. Were I using this, I'd use something else. If at all possible, I'd use anything else. If I couldn't, then I'd use whatever my rifle shot most accurately.

### 5.56

The real-deal stuff is marked XM193, made by Federal. It is 55-grain FMJ ammo that is loaded right to 5.56 pressures.

Yes, this is the successor to the original, M193 Vietnam-era ammo. However, compared to the (relatively) sedate velocities of ammo then, and most 55-grain FMJ now, the new stuff is run right to the redline. I have clocked lots of XM193 at well over 3200 fps, some close to 3300, out of a 20-inch rifle. If you didn't have to worry about barriers, it works great. And, it also works just fine from slow-twist barrels on up to the fast-twist mil-spec barrels.

The effectiveness comes from the wound track. The 55-grain bullet, on impact, begins to yaw. (Most bullets do; it's just that a lot of them do so slowly, and have exited before they can do any significant yawing.) Once it reaches a certain angle of yaw, the bullet breaks in half at the cannelure, and the two halves go their separate ways. The wound track of the front half, which by then

The Mk318 round the USMC is testing. This is what you can expect from a non-bonded bullet. The petals and lead core came apart, and this wasn't even in a barrier test.

has flattened somewhat, "J" hooks, that is, the nose of the bullet often curves off the direction of impact.

If you want to minimize penetration indoors, the XM193 is a good choice. It will break up on interior walls much faster than the "barrier-blind" bullets we'll be discussing and much better than any handgun round.

If what you want is accuracy, XM193 will shoot up to the quality of your barrel. Despite assertions by some, 1:7 twist barrels do not "scatter shots all over the target frame." I've shot plenty of sub-moa groups with

The gold standard for many years: the Federal Tactical bonded bullet.

This bullet went through auto glass and still held together and penetrated more than a foot of ballistic gel.

XM193, and have no problems dumping 300-meter computer pop-ups with it.

The choice is simple: there is only the one source, Federal, made in the Lake City ammo plant. Your choice is limited to production lot, which is inked on the box.

### M855

The much-maligned "green tip" ammo, it was developed to defeat Soviet body armor of the 1980s (which never appeared, by the way). It is essentially the 55-grain bullet with a 10-grain steel penetrator tip parked on top of the lead core, inside the jacket. It came about from experiments in the early 1980s to develop longer-range and better-penetrating 5.56 ammunition. Longer than the 55-grain FMJ, it requires a faster twist. 1:9 will do the job, but the rifles it is commonly fired from usually feature a 1:7 twist, creating some problems. Commonly derided because it "doesn't tumble," it actually does what it was designed to do, and does reasonably well: it punches holes in armor. The problems arise from the light weight of the steel part. Ten grains. And yes, it does tumble, just like the XM193, but the onset is delayed, and by the time it tumbles, it has already (usually) passed through the intended target.

If you're shooting people who are morbidly obese, it will have time to tumble. Thwacking skinny Somalis in Mogadishu, it hadn't time/people to tumble, hence the bad rep. A rep which continues to this day, since we're again shooting relatively under-nourished people in a part of the world where heavy clothing is not always the norm.

Accuracy with M855 is variable. If the production lot you're shooting has the steel tips well-centered, it shoots well. If not, it is maybe 2-moa ammo. Only testing will tell for the bunch you bought.

Given a choice, I would not use M855, simply because there are better choices.

### Remington PSP

The 55-grain pointed soft point is the standard load for a lot of entry teams. They want reasonable penetration on people, but as much non-penetration of walls as they can get. The lighter-constructed varmint bullets expand too quickly and don't provide proper wound tracks. However, if you are in a heavily-built area, with lots of people, you may want to consider it.

A friend of mine runs a large, multi-city SWAT team. Basically, he is a law enforcement officer who commands a light infantry company. When one of the cities in their jurisdiction was going to tear down an entire suburban-type neighborhood (for improvement I recall) they received permission to go in and do live-fire actual world testing on the buildings. What they found scared them. Any handgun round, and almost all shotgun projectiles (slugs and buckshot) would exit any building they were in unless it hit a sewer pipe or junction box. Masonry exteriors kept bullets in, but every room would be perforated.

The Remington PSP would not exit a building unless the first wall struck was an exterior wall and lacked masonry.

So, if you want to minimize penetration, and still want reasonable terminal ballistics, this is the one.

### M855LF

The first attempt at a lead-free bullet for the US Army, this was just the M855 with the lead core replaced by a non-lead composition. It didn't do anything better than the M855 did, and some experimen-

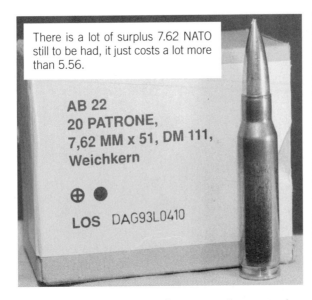

There is a lot of surplus 7.62 NATO still to be had, it just costs a lot more than 5.56.

AB 22
20 PATRONE,
7,62 MM x 51, DM 111,
Weichkern

LOS DAG93L0410

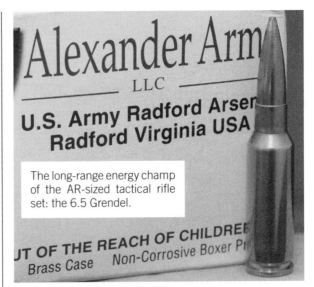

The long-range energy champ of the AR-sized tactical rifle set: the 6.5 Grendel.

tal compositions were not only exotic and expensive but proved to be disastrously more lethal than lead could ever be. No, I'm not kidding. The early attempts were done with a core composed of a tungsten-tin mixture. Well, in doing their due diligence, the testers surgically placed fragments of this compound into lab rats. In short order, they had cancer-ridden lab rats. You can imagine the consternation amongst the tree-hugging set. "Holy cow, we can't use this. If the Geneva Convention bans expanding bullets, what would they say about cancer-causing bullets?" (Actually, it's the Hague Accords that ban such bullets. So sue me.)

The irony of environmentally-friendly bullets actually causing cancer was not lost on those of us reading the summaries. The core composition was quickly changed to a different compound, of tin and bismuth, but the results were equally anti-climactic, if not ironic; they were just bullets. And since the Army was willing to knuckle under to the environmentalists if it got them better bullets, but not if it only got them stuff that was "just as good", it got passed over.

You might see some of this as individual collector's items, (the later, non-tungsten stuff, not the early ammo) and then again you might never see a round in your lifetime. No need to seek it out for shooting.

### M855A1

Also known as M855A1 EPR, for enhanced performing ammunition, the "A1" is catching a lot of flak because it is perceived as the Army bowing to the "greenies." That is, there is no lead in the bullet. It features a larger steel core than the M855, and the base is composed of a bismuth/tin compound. The steel tip of

the "A1" is, unlike the M855, exterior to the jacket. In the M855, the tip is inside, and ahead of the lead core. On the M855A1, the steel tip is just like the plastic ballistic tip on hunting bullets; it pokes up out of the jacket.

The M855A1 was intended to improve barrier penetration for our troops in Iraq, who would more often than they liked find themselves frantically hosing oncoming vehicles (and unarmored ones at that) only to find that none of the shots that hit made it into the passenger compartment.

The flak comes from repeated attempts of the environmental crowd to ban lead in bullets. If the Army is making better ammo, great, but to bow to the greenies over bullets is too much for some to bear.

For our purposes, it takes a bad bullet and makes it worse. The bigger steel tip makes it a better penetrator, but for most applications we don't want extra penetration without also getting some expansion. As for accuracy, what few reports I've received have it the same as M855; it depends on which lot you're using.

As with the M855, if it was all I had to work with, I'd use it. But given a choice of just about anything, I'd go with something else.

### Mk 262 Mod 1

The origins of this load came from target ammo: specifically, the heaviest bullet that could be magazine-fed from an AR. That maxed out at 75 to 77 grains. Taking one of those bullets and loading it to the maximum pressure a 5.56 case could stand, the results were impressive. Very good speed (heavier bullets than these, which had to be seated deeper in the case, lost

The Asym all-copper bullet, showing perfect performance in ballistic gel.

The Cor-bon all-copper bullet, with its petals and core, after auto glass and heavy clothing combined barrier test.

impressive amounts of velocity, so no gain there). Superb accuracy, and due to the low drag, better retained velocity at distance. While M855 was accurate enough to tag people at 600 yards, the Mk 262 carried more speed out there. What it didn't do was use that energy effectively at extreme range.

To get an XM193-like action, and also provide a place to crimp the case neck, the Mod 1 (the old ammo became known as Mk 262 Mod 0) gained a cannelure. That allowed for bullet break-up due to yaw at impressive distances. Where the XM193 and the M855 can fail to break up at distances (depending on the barrel length launched from) of 75 to 200 yards, the Mk 262 Mod 1 will break up past 300 meters.

How can it do this, with less starting velocity? Simple: leverage. The longer 77-grain bullet presents a longer lever to the resistance of the ballistic gel it passes through, when it overturns. As Archimedes said; "Give me a long enough lever and I can move the earth." Give me a long enough bullet, and I can break it at low velocities. Break-up happens quickly in gel and continues to happen out to the "normal" combat distances.

As far as accuracy is concerned, you'll need a 1:7 barrel (or a 1:8 match tube) and with it the load will shoot as well as you can, for as far as you can see and hold.

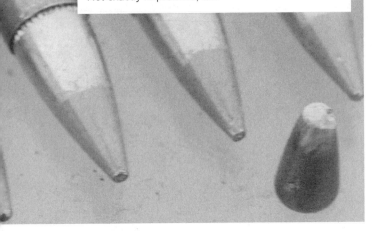

The steel penetrator tip, from inside the M855 round. Not exactly impressive, eh?

This load is made in relatively small lots for the military, and getting your hands on some will not be easy. And it gains bullet break-up at the expense of penetration. This is not a "barrier-blind" bullet. For barrier-blind bullets, we have to go elsewhere.

### Mk318

The USMC was not at all happy with the Army's selection of the M855A1. (And if you do a search for "M318" be prepared to learn a whole lot about 90mm tank gun ammo.) I acquired a small supply from Federal, who box it as "T556TNB1" but everyone calls it Mk 318 Mod 0. The bullet is a solid-copper base and nose, with a small, non-bonded lead tip. The balance should mean good accuracy and terminal performance. However, testing was not all peaches 'n' cream.

The non-bonded lead core up front will not stay attached to the copper once the bullet hits. Ballistic gelatin, water, intermediate barriers, the tip expands (not because it was designed to, but as an incidental result of the manufacturing process) and the lead core peels off, while the petals get shed. The result is a solid copper slug that continues to penetrate. Why all this folderol? Simple; an all-copper bullet does nothing for the Marines. A bullet with a lead tip remains point-on, for accuracy and penetration. But the lack of bonding mostly defeats bullet enhancement.

As far as accuracy is concerned, if the USMC was no happy with the M855A1, they are not going to be any more pleased with the Mk 318. I shot the small amount I had to test on the same day, with the same rifles, I was punching sub-MOA groups with Mk 262 Mod 1 ammo. The groups with Mk 318 always had at least one flyer, and sometimes two. What could have been an MOA group always turned into a 2+ MOA group. I can't see Marines settling for ammo that is less accurate than M855.

Again, if it was what I had, I'd use it, but I'd want something else. I figure the USMC is going to use it (since they paid to have it developed) only as long as it takes to come up with a bullet that works the way they want, and at the accuracy level they depend on.

### Federal Tactical Bonded

One of the originals, the Federal Tactical Bonded uses a bullet that is, simply, a lead core soldered into a copper jacket. The process is simple, but details matter, and there is a lot of hand-assembly involved. Picture little old ladies sitting at a bench, laboriously inserting little lead cores into arrays of upright copper jackets. You got it. The assemblies are then heated, and the two are soldered together.

A Tactical Bonded bullet, striking gel or a barrier, does not shed its jacket. It can't. What it does is hold together, and continue on through the barrier, the gel, whatever is in the way. It expands, but the expansion is not always the picture-perfect "mushroom" that the art department likes to see.

What you gain, you can't undo. Where a Remington PSP, or an XM193 will break up on interior walls, the Tactical Bonded just keeps on going. So, if you are a state trooper, working around cars all the time, it is the greatest thing since Otto Frederick Rohwedder invented sliced bread. If you are at home, and worried about what is on the other side of the wall, it is not so good.

As for accuracy, the Tactical Bonded is never going to sweep the line at Camp Perry. It struggles to get down to 1 MOA, but it isn't meant to be long-range lightweight sniper ammo.

The bonded bullet approach has gained such favor with the FBI that pretty much everyone makes it, or something like it, today. It is very expensive, but if you are going to be working around vehicles, or are not concerned about over-penetration in structures, it is very good to have.

### Asym TSX

While Asym offers several loads, the TSX is what we're after here. Using the Barnes 70-grain TSX bullet, it does all the hard parts: it shoots accurately, it penetrates to a fare-thee-well, and it expands. It does not, however, break up on interior walls. No barrier-blind load will do that, at least not until we make ammunition with microscopic microprocessors in each projectile.

The TSX is an all-copper bullet, with a hollow tip and pre-cut petals. On ballistic gelatin it expands completely and reliably. On barriers, it punches through, then continues on a straight line through gel. Some barriers slow the expansion, some barriers shred them off the core. But the core continues. Designed to expand, the TSX will do so even at velocities as low as 2,000 fps. That means, even with an SBR, you're going to get expansion past 200 yards.

Accuracy? As much as your rifle can deliver, up to your skill level. Of course, the long 70-grain all-copper bullet will require a twist no slower than 1:8 to stabilize the bullet.

Cor-Bon has been making the same kind of ammo for a few years. What you have to keep in mind is that an all-copper bullet will be longer than one with a lead core. As a result, you have to be very careful about barrel twist when using such bullets. While some heavier than 55-grain lead-core bullets will stabilize in a 1:12

barrel, no all-copper bullets will.

## Medium-Bores

Here we have the 6.8, the 6.5 and the 7.62X39. While ballistically similar, they work in different ways and for different purposes.

### 6.8 Remington SPC

Developed by Special Forces NCOs, the idea was simple: to get the biggest bang out of an M4 package as possible, with the least modifications necessary. The base case is the .30 Remington, shortened and necked down to 6.8. The result is a clone of the .276 Pedersen, which the Army considered and didn't adopt all the way back in 1936. It is very good at what it does, and it does it well and reliably.

What limits adoption is limited adoption. The circular logic goes like this: it works great, but until it gets adopted by some big agency, it won't become popular enough to receive widespread adoption. And it won't be considered by an agency because it hasn't been widely accepted. Nobody said we gun-guys were consistent or

A barrier-blind bullet holds together through barriers, and still expands in ballistic gelatin. This Remington bonded bullet shows what modern designers have come up with.

even entirely rational.

Given the 6.8 as the round to use, I'd settle on Hornady 110-grain BTHP, which opens well, and still has enough mass to work well even if it doesn't open.

### 6.5 Grendel

Designed by Bill Alexander, the 6.5 Grendel has as its parent case the 7.62X39. Blown out, necked down and given a sharp shoulder, it is the best long-range medium bore to be had. It uses a 123-grain Lapua Scenar bullet, at 2500 fps or so, which bullet stays supersonic well past 1,000 yards. As a close-range thumper it is great. As a long-range poker with light recoil, it excels even more.

Using it, I'd stick with the 123-grain Scenar.

### 7.62X39

The classic AK round, it is the vanilla plain cartridge of the rifle world. There is no lack of surplus (and semi-surplus) ammo, and it is all pretty much the same, a 123-grain FMJ, moving along at somewhere around 2300 fps.

What ammo? Whatever is available. Some will argue the merits of this or that, claiming that the Yugoslavian lead-core round is faster at tumbling and thus the best. Me, I don't expect any AK bullet to tumble, and expect them all to simply poke .30 caliber holes through objects.

## Big Bores

There really is only one: the 7.62X51 NATO round.

### 7.62X51

Surplus abounds, although it is pricey. The basic load is a 147-grain FMJ, at 2700 fps out of a full-length barrel. You can get heavier, up to the M118LR, a 175-grain match boattail bullet, meant for long-range sniper use. None will expand, some might tumble, and a very few will fragment.

It was with some embarrassment back in the Vietnam war era, when many European countries were hectoring us about our fragmenting .223 round, for them to find their 7.62 was doing the same. They had made bullets with thinner and thinner jackets (probably as an economy measure) until they found that the jackets were thin enough to allow fragmentation. And in the exact same process as our .223, with its 55-grain bullet.

The ammo is now hard to find, and it exists only in particular lots of particular years of production, but if you search you can find it.

For the rest of us, the heavy bullet at speed is plenty good enough. Surplus comes in German, British, Indian, Argentine and odd lots of other countries. The thing to do is this: find some at a good price. Try it. If it shoots well, and reasonably accurately, buy as much as you can stand. Don't buy a garage full until you've tested it. I have a batch of Radway Green (British-made, for their L1A1 FAL) that works fine in my FALs, but not particularly accurately. In some of my other .308s, the ammo is horrid, causing malfunctions and shooting with poor accuracy. I bought it for $50 per thousand rounds, and at that price I'm willing to keep it away from my M1As, CETME, etc. (and yes, it was a long time ago).

The other extreme is precision ammo. Here, you find what works most accurately in your sniper rifle and stock up. This stuff will probably cost you $750 per thousand rounds.

What to use? Whatever gets the job done. Here, you have enough mass and speed that bullet construction is a lesser consideration.

## Update

I had someone ask; "OK, what is this barrier-blind stuff? It doesn't see the wall?" No, the idea, first promulgated by the FBI (although not so explicitly) in their ballistic testing, is that a bullet should perform after it has passed through a barrier, as if there had been no barrier there. That is, it should expand regardless of what it has had to pass through. This, it turns out, is actually easier with handgun bullets than it is with rifle bullets. The very aspects of rifles that make them so much more useful in a defensive situation are the very things that work against them; speed and bullet toughness.

It is easy to get a bullet through a barrier: make the jacket or the core (or both) tougher, and pointy. To get it to expand, you want to do just the opposite. So, to make a rifle bullet that both zips through a barrier, and still expands when it penetrates ballistic gel (or people) is the holy grail.

To describe a bullet that did just that, we had to come up with a new name: barrier-blind. I probably would not have come up with this one, but now that it has come into relatively common use, we're stuck with it.

# The SIG 556

The SIG 556, aka the Stg90, has been rightly called "An AK built to Swiss watch standards." It is a long-stroke piston system that is clearly derived from the AK, although nothing will interchange. It took longer for the Swiss to switch to the 5.56 from a .30 rifle, for one simple reason: every man in Switzerland is a member of the Army. Barring some medical or theological reason, every man undergoes military training upon reaching maturity and is a member of the Reserves for the rest of his adult life afterwards. As such, he has to shoot a qualifying score annually.

In this regard the Swiss are a lot like the USMC. You can bet that the Marine General who is a member of the Joint Chiefs of Staff gets his butt out to the rifle range at least once a year and with a rack-grade M16 shoots a passing or better score. In Switzerland, every adult male has to do the same, regardless of profession. (I've heard that the Swiss diplomatic staff here in the US get themselves to an appropriate range and shoot a score annually. I don't know what they do in other countries.)

The course is simple, but not easy. It is a bullseye target at 300 meters. It is shot prone, with a bipod support, and iron sights. Switzerland is dotted with 300-meter ranges, many of them quite comfortably appointed, with weather covers, downrange cameras and instant scoring systems. You may ask why? Why 300 meters, and why prone from a bipod? Because Switzerland is a country of long-standing origins, and every inch of it is surveyed, known and plotted.

The mountain passes have fighting emplacements for riflemen, machine gunners, mortar teams and pre-positioned artillery. If you were to pop yourself into a foxhole overlooking a mountain pass, you'd find that is it camoflaged to the point of practically being landscaped, the foxhole being made of concrete and range cards to all the prominent points of interest. A Swiss rifleman would be in there, with his rifle on its bipod, basically sniping at the enemy infantry as it tried to move through terrain where every tree, every corner of a building is a known distance, to within a fraction of a meter.

The Swiss did not want to give up their precision .30 rifles for something that would not only hurt their qual scores, but also hinder them in long-range hosing of obstinate infantrymen. Once they had a 5.56 rifle that was suitably accurate at 300 meters, they adopted it.

The SIG 556 is handy, controllable, and accurate. You would expect no less from the Swiss.

The beauty of a piston design is the relative ease with which designers can modify it into a short-barreled rifle.

Is shooting fun? Yes. Is shooting a short-barreled rifle more fun? Guess.

Even in the Federally-mandated 16-inch barrel, the SIG 556 is a handy rifle.

Set up as a DMR, the SIG 556 is scarily accurate.

The original design used an AR stock, which did not go over as well as hoped. SIG switched to the original design as quickly as they could.

The trigger parts are nothing like the AR's, and you would be best to not take them apart.

The 556's 1:7 twist will handle all the usual suspects when it comes to ammo.

RESTRICTED FOR LAW ENFORCEMENT/GOVERNMENT USE AND/OR EXPORT ONLY

S

5.56MM
BALL XM
10 RD C
SMQ07

The piston system rides in the guide tube, above the barrel.

The 556 lacks the selector that travels to three locations, a detail that we'll have to get used to.

SIG 556 5.56 NATO, SIG SAUER INC, EXETER, NH, USA

JS 028496

The Swiss take preparedness seriously. Here is standard-issue (albeit 7.5mm) ammo for home storage.

The 556 we have here in the US today differs in some significant ways. First of all, it is built here, and it is semi-auto only. No select-fire rifles, unless your department is buying them for you. Second, the magazines are different. The original rifle was made in time for some few to be imported before President Bush the First mis-used executive privilege to slam shut the importation of rifles. Those rifles used the Swiss magazines. When word came out that SIG was going to be making the 556, the owners of those rifles practically leapt for joy. More magazines! You see, they hadn't been able to get new mags for 20 years, since importation of the rifles had been stopped. The dribs and drabs of magazine availability dried up completely with the Assault Weapons Ban of 1994. Well, SIG took a look at the market and decided that while the Swiss mags worked well, building the rifle here but using the Swiss magazines would hinder sales. So they made the new rifle so it accepted standard M16/AR-15 magazines.

The piston, carrier, bolt and charging handle, out of the rifle. Easy to clean.

The hinged lever on the bolt carrier is the latch that allows removal of the charging handle.

The new stock style both folds and adjusts for length of pull.

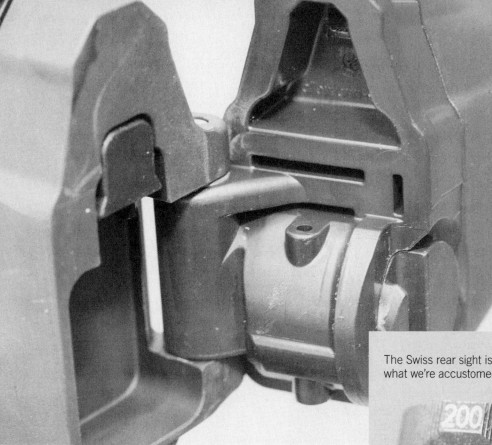

The stock latches securely, and hinges out of the way when stored or in a vehicle.

The Swiss rear sight is elaborate, precise, and not at all what we're accustomed to in the AR-verse.

While this was a disappointment to the owners of the classic rifles, it was a smart move, as the supply of AR mags is so great that it is approaching one for every man, woman and child in the US.

Another choice they made did not go over so well. SIG at first made the stock extension a standard mil-spec buffer tube dimension, so it would work with any AR-15 stock. It folded, like the Swiss ones did, but it had an AR-15 back end. That wasn't so well received, and it didn't take long for the stock to be changed to the "proper" Swiss design.

The SIG 556 is, as I said, a long-stroke piston system. The carrier is very much like the AK's, if one can say that a Mercedes is very much like a Yugo. It is, however, a two-piece design, to accommodate the recoil spring. There are differences apart from the quality of manufacture, The charging handle of the SIG is held in place by a spring-loaded lever. That allows you to remove the charging handle and thus allows the Swiss (and now SIG USA) to make the upper receiver as a steel tube instead of merely a cover over the lower.

That changes the upper/lower relationship, so it is much more like an AR than an AK, in that the upper and the barrel are one unit, and the lower, with the internals and buttstock, is another. Also, the front of the gas system has a regulator, so you can adjust for adverse conditions, unlike the "one setting for all" AK system.

The barrel is a cold hammer-forged and chrome-lined barrel with a 5.56 chamber and a 1:7 twist. With the fast twist, and the 5.56 chamber, it will handle even heavy bullets in the hottest mil-spec loads. The Classic has a Swiss-style forearm and buttstock, and the stock both folds and is adjustable for length of pull. The SIG-made AR-15 pattern magazines clip together so you can have two or three all in one package, ready for quick reloads. Remember the description above, of a Swiss infantryman dealing with an invasion? He's going to be in a solid fighting position, hosing infantry at medium to long range, and with two or three loaded magazines he can really dish it out before he has to relocate to a different position.

I had a chance to visit the SIG plant in New Hampshire and shoot the 556 in both semi and select-fire versions, full-size and SBR. At a smidge over eight pounds it certainly is not a thumper in recoil, and controlling bursts was no big deal. Accuracy was everything you'd expect from a Swiss rifle, and for the day's shooting, neither the other shooters nor I had any malfunctions.

Inasmuch as the 556 is a long-stroke piston, its ejection is rather brisk, but it is not at all hard on the brass and does not approach the level of violence that an HK rifle demonstrates.

The selector is ambidextrous, and is low-profile enough that it does not interfere with my firing grip.

If you want an ultra-reliable rifle, with plenty of accuracy, and you don't want to have "another AR" like your buddies at the gun club, the SIG 556 is an option you should consider.

The gas regulator adjusts gas flow, for adverse conditions or no gas.

# Sniper Rifles

The classic image we have of snipers is that of a lone shooter, or one with a steady companion, waiting in silence in a jungle, or in a ruined building, peering through a scope. Watching patiently, he finally sees his quarry pause, and squeezing the trigger, makes the shot from an impossible distance – so far away that those around the now-retired target don't know which direction the shot came from, or where to direct their response.

I had a Special Forces trained sniper once tell me "life begins at the triple zero." Meaning, it was best to work at 1,000 yards or more.

This image has so distorted the reality that just getting things done properly became a problem. For instance, the classic Army and USMC sniper rifle was a Remington bolt gun, called the M40 in the Corps, and the M24 in the Army, chambered in .308. On top was a scope of 10X, 10 power, with a mil-dot ranging reticle in it. With it, the school-trained snipers could estimate range (using the surveying ability of the mil-dot reticle) and poke holes in targets out as far as the bullet was stable. (More on that in a bit.)

Well, when it came time for the police to adopt some kind of counter-sniper rifle, and training, guess what they used as their base? Yes, the .308 bolt gun with 10X scope. Now take a guess, a wild guess, at the average distance of police counter-sniper shots? I'll wait while you ponder the question. Ready? 53 yards. That's right, the maximum distance we used to be shooting handguns at, and some still do, is the average for a scoped rifle, from a rest, for police. Now, imagine what the field of view is through a 10X scope at 53 yards. Pretty small.

Why such a short distance? A few things: for one, most distances in urban areas just aren't that far apart. Oh, you can see a building 600 yards away, but SWAT isn't going to set up a perimeter that far out. They haven't the manpower. Second, no police chief, sheriff, SWAT commander or watch commander who has to say yes or no to a shot (commonly referred to as "the green light") is going to give the nod to anything other than a last-moment shot, at the closest possible range. Picking someone off at 600 yards would be quickly followed by a raft of lawsuits (which are going to happen anyway, things being what they are in the modern world) and pilloried for the decision.

Now, that is not always the case. The Texas Tower incident, where Charles Whitman climbed to the top of the bell tower on the U-T/Austin campus, was a long-range affair. He was on the 29th floor observation deck, and he made successful shots out past 400 yards. His efforts were greatly hampered by the residents going home, getting hunting rifles, and returning fire. (I cannot imagine such a thing happening today. The first police to arrive then, joined in. Today, they'd be arresting those firing back, even if it meant getting shot by the "guy in the tower." Such is modern life.) But back to the modern police and military perspective:

What if you, the police precision marksman, need a follow-up shot? Well, for the military shooter, planning on whacking a general at 1,000+ yards, "follow-up" is anything they do before the chopper picks them up. For a police officer, follow-up is what you need to do before the felon falls to the ground, and still tries to fire the weapon he has in his hands.

When we went into Iraq, things seemed to go as planned. In the wide-open spaces, long range was desired, and snipers were expected to work as they normally would. But one of the things a lot of critics don't seem to get about combat is the interactive nature of it. It isn't like a video game, where "level seventeen" is always the same.

A lot of those who think we can create peace, love and understanding by means of talk, good intentions and proper PR seem to think that combat (or law enforcement, for that matter) is like a video game. If you know what will happen on level 17, then you can cruise right through. And each time you have to go through 17 on the way to 18, 19 and 20, the "bad guys" in level 17 will do the same thing. I can only imagine that people with such a child-like view of the world have never even experienced so much as a fistfight in the grade school playground.

Combat is more like football: you go in with a plan. If it works, you keep doing it. If it doesn't, you change. If the other guy finds what he's doing isn't working, he'll change. Oh, in the case of a lot of the insurgents, they refused to change, and got shot for their efforts. Ideology, political or religious, can prevent change. But once the stupid or stubborn ones are killed off (and let's be clear and blunt about this; we're talking combat) then those that are left will change. Adapt. Find what works, or at least works better.

Which is what happened in Iraq. After standing up and slugging it out, the bad guys figured out that IEDs worked better. So, they started setting bombs. Our guys adapted by changing the doctrine of how snipers worked.

Previously, snipers worked in two-man teams. (And, lest you think I'm revealing state secrets, this is common knowledge amongst those who pay attention.) They worked for commanders higher in the food chain than platoon or company commanders. Even battalion honchos were out of the loop at times. Snipers early on were viewed as being just as valuable if they saw and reported good intel as they were if they whacked bad guys. A sniper who is "working for" the regimental commander won't even have a way to talk to the

Snipers traditionally worked in pairs: one shooter, one spotter. Recent experience has forced some changes in that.

Snipers and rooftops, together for a reason: you need to see an area in order to control it. U.S. Marine Corps Sgt. Rick Keller in Helmand Province. DoD photo by Lance Cpl. Tommy Bellegarde, U.S. Marine Corps.

What everyone thinks of as a sniper, with a bolt gun and a 10X scope. Here, Lance Corporals Lawson and Press decide what order they will drill approaching Taliban in Helmand Province. DoD photo by Sgt. Brian A. Tuthill, U.S. Marine Corps.

company commander whose area he's "hunting in." Barring an emergency, or a need to not get shot at by his own guys, the sniper would not even talk to, or be known to, the company commander.

The Iraqi-based bad guys started setting IEDs, and snipers went out with the idea of getting into a good "hide" and either shooting or reporting on the bomb setters. Well, when you're out there on your own, two-man teams are less than optimal. In fact, they're stupid. Two guys can't watch the possible bomb sites and simultaneously watch their own backs. And if the bad guys come for them (someone spotted them, someone figured out the likely locations for hides, etc.) two guys can't hold off more than a handful of attackers. Especially if one of them has a bolt-action M40/24.

Because bolt guns are slow. Oh, a trained bolt-gunner can fire 10 aimed shots in 70 second at Camp Perry, but that didn't help. You see, school-trained snipers aren't trained to work a bolt as if they were on the line at Perry. And 70 seconds is forever. If a team shows up to set a bomb, you want to bag them all, not just one

or two. A bolt-gunner can get one, maybe two if they are far from cover. If someone has you under fire from an adjacent building while their buddies are assaulting up the staircase that is your exit, 70 seconds may be the rest of your life. As a result, there is a big push in the services for a semi-automatic sniper rifle and for bigger sniper teams.

You see, the bad guys were no dummies. An IED wasn't just a-guy-with-a-shovel-and-a-satchel affair. Proper location mattered. So, once they'd scouted out a good spot, there would be a team on the job: the explosives expert (or what passed for one, given the time and place), the digger or diggers, the security team, spotters and so on. Anywhere from four to 10 guys. Clearly, it would be expeditious to bag all of them. That way, the skilled/experienced ones will be removed from the lists, to be replaced by less-experienced ones. Also, it becomes a lot more difficult to recruit new bomb-team members, if each time a team gets "made" they all get shot.

Now, on the sniper end of things, it becomes more

difficult and involved. First, you can't send out just a two-man team. Once things shifted to a sniper-vs.-bombers basis sending two-man teams out was a good way of ensuring they didn't come back. So, it became a team job. A team would be three or more pairs of sniper-spotters with another handful of security members. You could have a dozen men trying to sneak through the streets, set up, and watch unobserved, to cover a likely bomb area or areas. The bigger the group, the more difficult it was to insert the team and pass unnoticed. And the team needed a bigger area, as you couldn't just pack a dozen guys (and all their gear) into a small corner room of an apartment building.

The snipers also had another problem: gear. If you're going to whack bad guys at distance, you need a bolt gun with a 10X scope. (And remember, the guys doing this were limited to the tools in inventory. No fair in saying "they should have been using XYZ rifle. The government didn't have any.) But an M24 is not what you need if the team gets spotted on the way in and you find yourself in a fight to extricate yourselves from the mess. For that you need an M4. So, what to do? Pack everything? An M24, ammo, spotting scope, shooting mat, etc. and an M4 with a go-bag full of loaded magazines? Even if you're a twenty-something trooper in peak physical condition, that's a lot of stuff to be humping.

So a semi-auto sniper rifle becomes very attractive. Especially if you can swap uppers. For the insertion part, you'd be cat-footing in with a 14.5-inch .308 rifle and an Aimpoint or EOTech on it. The short length and the no-magnification optics mean you'd be using a fast and nimble hammer on the tangos across the street, the ones who stumbled into your team while you were heading to the objective. If you don't get spotted and you make it to your intended area, you have time to set up. Once in place, you take that upper off, and pull the 20-incher with 10X scope upper out of your rucksack. Now you're set to get the job done at 600 yards and more.

Now, this is not a problem that is new. When the repeating rifle with smokeless powder, was new, suddenly riflemen had range. They could dependably hit a man-sized target at impressive distances (on the target

The changes in use have caused official interest in .308 self-loading sniper rifles. Here is the DPMS REPR getting a workout.

The military is moving from just bolt guns to adding semi-auto (and select-fire) sniper rifles. This is a LWRCI REPR, done up in flat dark earth.

range, anyway) compared to what the black powder rifles of the time could do. As a result, rifles were set up for distance. Common military sights of the time, when set at their lowest setting, would produce bullet impacts 6 to 8 to 10 inches over the point of aim at 100 yards. The idea was simple: hold your sights on the belt buckle of the opposing soldier, and at any distance out to combat maximum, in some cases well past 400 yards, you'd get a hit. Beyond that, you'd then adjust your sights for range.

In WWI, with the trenches 100 yards apart or so, you have to figure a lot of soldiers were guessing as to how much under they had to hold, to get a hit.

Even in WWII, with a lot of wide-open areas, most engagements were at relatively close distances. Much sniper work was done in the ruins of the various cities on the Eastern Front, as the Soviets pushed the Germans back. Even when the fight was in the wide open steppes, the shots were often just a few hundred yards or less, since the first order of getting a decisive shot is to spot the target. If you can't see him, you can't shoot him. It is rare that range becomes the only issue in the mix of variables.

In another instance of the interactive nature of combat, Major Thomas Ehrhart in his monograph "Increasing Small Arms Lethality in Afghanistan" reports on the adaptation of the Taliban combatants. The average US soldier is not trained to shoot beyond 300 meters. That's the maximum distance of the computer-controlled pop-up targets he or she shoots at. (Marines shoot on ranges longer than that, but only to 500 meters.) Worse yet, since a soldier only gets 20 rounds for 20 targets in the qual course, they are routinely told to ignore the 300- and 275-meter targets and save those shots for the closer targets to ensure a hit, and thus a passing score. (Passing is 12 out of 20, or 24 out of 40), so a Taliban at 400 meters is relatively safe from most Army shooters.

The minimum distance at which artillery, air strikes, naval gunfire (probably not an issue in Afghanistan) or a Spectre gunship can fire is not as close as you'd think. As a courtesy to those providing indirect fire support, the requester will mention when things are particularly troublesome at the moment, with bad guys at a close range: the fire request will include the term "danger close." Basically that means "For what you're sending, we're at or inside the minimum safe distance the field manual calls for. Please be careful."

How close is "close?" Well, the calculated minimum (it involves the average dispersion of fired rounds, the distance fired, the standard deviation of fragment spread and distance traveled, and for all I know, the phase of the moon) are listed in various field manuals. What I've been advised are working distances are as follows:

M203 & Mk19 100 meters
60mm mortars 200 meters
81mm mortar 300 meters
120mm mortar 600 meters
105mm 750 meters
155 & larger 1,000 meters

You'll note that while the organic firepower that a squad, platoon or company might posses will cover past the 300 meter range, the larger stuff leaves a gap. Also be aware of a small detail, but an important one: the minimum safe distance depends to a certain degree on the distance to the artillery battery, i.e., time of flight.

The police took their lead from the military, and it is a good thing the Barrett wasn't in use when the police started. Here, U.S. Marine Corps Lance Cpl. Mark Trent covers the area from a recently-captured compound in Afghanistan. DoD photo by Lance Cpl. Tommy Bellegarde, U.S. Marine Corps.

The military has been more interested in the GPMG, here an M240, than in fielding sniper rifles and training soldiers to use them. Here, Seabees train with the M240 Bravo. DoD photo by Petty Officer 2nd Class Ace Rheaume, U.S. Navy.

For fast follow-up shots, a bolt gun loses every time to a self-loader. Here, they're just watching suspicious activity on Highway 1 in Zabul Province. DoD photo by Spc. Joshua Grenier, U.S. Army.

For the police, a bolt-action still is useful, at least, until we have to deal with IED-setting teams here.

The longer a projectile is in the air, the longer air currents can work on it. A mortar firing "charge zero" (the minimum the things will fly) will be dropping shells only a hundred yards or more downrange. For that, "danger close" could be 20 yards, if you really trust the mortar gunner to know his stuff. Time of flight is just a few seconds. A big gun, such as a 155mm, or an eight-inch howitzer, can have a flight time of more than a minute at their maximum range. For that transit time, you want to have them start far out, and work their way closer.

Now, the calculated safe minimum instance, and the one actually in effect by careful troops who are depending on well-trained support is a lot less. But you still won't see 155s coming in on a hilltop 5-600 meters away, not on a regular basis, not first rounds, and not unless it is a real emergency.

There's also the matter of time. If a savvy small unit leader has planned ahead, he will have already picked likely hilltops and such on the map, places that might be useful to shoot at his unit. If he has done so, and coordinated with the local artillery battery, they can speed things up. The artillery battery can have the guns laid on each position in sequence, as the infantry unit approaches it. They can have pre-calculated the firing solution and have rounds one step from ready. If he does that (and the artillery unit is willing to go to the constant work involved) he can easily have shells on target starting one minute after calling for fire.

If he hasn't, but the battery is ready and waiting, and he has a good forward observer, the first ones will hit in three or four minutes, and adjusted and hammered soon after. From a cold start, with guns not registered, and scrambling to re-lay the gun, it can be 10 minutes or more before you have hot steel raining down on your problem du jour.

One minute is a long time, four an eternity. If the Taliban are smart (and at least some of them have to

be) then a smart guy will have his ambush team fully trained and instructed. In one minute, an ambusher can have two full belts downrange from each machine gun, two or three rounds from each RPG, and half a dozen or more rounds from a 60mm mortar. And then be packing and boogeying off the ridgeline before the first artillery round is incoming. Four minutes? He's out of the severe hazard zone, and almost in the next zip code.

Now, there's one wrinkle for the bad guys in this disparity between safe distance and ordnance: the Spectre gunship. For those who don't know about it, it came about as an improvement over "Puff the Magic Dragon" in Vietnam. That was a C-47 with a row of machine

In the mountains, where you might need range, a .308 rifle can be quite useful, Here Spc Rockwell scans the ridgeline. DoD photo by Spc. Eric Cabral, U.S. Army.

The British Ministry of Defence recently adopted the LMT .308 as the L129A1 sniper rifle.

A successful head shot at on a steel plate at 600 yards. Yes, this is fun.

guns (later, miniguns) pointing out the windows. The pilot would bank around a particular spot, and trigger the guns, and be firing a whole row of machineguns that would pour rounds into the area. The Spectre is simply a C-130 with miniguns, 25mm, 40mm cannons and a 105mm howitzer pointing out the left side. And as a vast improvement over the C-47, the C-130 pilot banks but the gun crew use video monitors to precisely refine aim and place shots where they need to be. I have heard from those who have been there that a Spectre can place its shots safely (after all, the distance involved is almost inconsequential by artillery terms) as close at 50 meters. That is, a circling Spectre can put a 105mm shell right through the window of the building across a boulevard from your position.

You're probably thinking "This means we can drop explosives where we want." Yes – but. The max speed of a C-130 is 260 knots (299 mph). However, it isn't going at max while banking and hammering. The speed there (it depends on altitude, gross weight, etc. ) is more like 150-175 mph. Which means it is a big, fat, slow-moving target for surface-to-air missiles. As a result, use of the C-130H and C-130J models are restricted to night-time use in Afghanistan.

Once they figured out there was a gap, the Taliban took advantage of this gap. Inside the artillery or air

Extending the magazine of a bolt action only delays the inevitable: it will always fall behind a self-loader for repeat shots.

strike danger zone, but outside of the effective rifle fire, the Taliban had only to worry about belt-fed machineguns, and the 7.62 ones at that. Yes, a sniper rifle would be very helpful, but it isn't exactly an even match: a bolt-action sniper rifle with a five-round magazine, vs. a belt-fed 7.62, on a tripod, at 800 meters, with belts of ammo ready, and a spotter to call the range.

Again, a semi-auto sniper rifle would be very useful in those instances.

You might be asking "Why not pack the mortars or grenade launchers?" Simple: they weigh a lot and can't be man-packed across much of a distance. The M224 60mm mortar, bipod, baseplate, tube and sight weighs 46.5 pounds, and each round weighs 3.75 pounds. The three-man crew can't carry it and any significant amount of ammo as well. So, if you plan on having a mortar and 20 rounds with you, you have to figure out how to pack an additional 150 pounds, once you account for the mortar and gear, plus the ammo and their packing tubes. (You do not pack bare mortar shells in your gear. Pack it in the storage tubes, or prepare to be shunned by all.)

In precision rifles, the magazines commonly feed from a central line, not from two sides of a box magazine. Double-stack mags are far easier to load, an item the military must consider.

The LWRCI REPRS, in the three barrel lengths I could obtain. The shortest would be an SBR, and that requires an NFA Tax Stamp.

The LWRCI REPR carbine, on the qual course. A few off the "X" count, which for me usually comes at the kneeling stage.

So you need an additional vehicle to haul the crew and mortar. Or a dedicated mortar team.

Now, imagine a Taliban commander, watching an approaching American convoy of up-armored Humvees. If he knows what the one with the mortar crew looks like, that's the one he'll instruct his best machine-gun crew to work over first. If not, as soon as he spots the crew setting up, guess who gets his attention? Ditto the vehicle armed with a Mk 19 grenade launcher. And if the convoy looks too tough, he'll just let them pass and clobber the next one.

And none of this helps a patrol on foot.

My apologies for giving you so much info on mortars, artillery and such, but I think it is important to understand the context in which the modern sniper works these days.

The US armed forces have been using a semi-auto for a while; the M110, a .308 semi-auto, also known as the Knight's SR-25, a descendant of the AR-10. While loved by some, it is also the recipient of some criticism. Across the Atlantic, the British recently adopted the L129A1, made by LMT.

Now, the effectiveness of a system is not just a matter of features, specs and cost. Training matters. In many instances, training can matter more than gear.

But, being the gearheads we are, we spend a lot of time looking at gear and features. So, let's get to it.

## LWRCI REPR

I had the great fortune to have them send me three version of the new, .308 rifle, one in each barrel length. Well, in each barrel length they could send me: 16, 18 and 20 inches. (No SBRs for your favorite scribe, alas.)

The REPR is a scaled-up AR-15 (which was itself a scaled-down AR-10) but there are parts in common, and accessories galore meant for your 5.56 will fit the 7.62 REPR. The controls and exterior features are all instantly recognizable and familiar to the 5.56 shooter. Well, most. Where the 5.56 has a charging handle on the rear of the upper receiver, the REPR has a charging handle on the left side. It is non-reciprocating, so it won't move when you shoot. It has a large knob, and if you press in (towards the rifle interior) on the knob, it engages the charging handle, and you can then use it as a forward assist. When you let go, the spring-loaded knob pops back out, ending its short tenure as an assistant.

Also, there are extra levers on the exterior. There are two bolts release levers, one on each side, so you can

The Blaser has adjustable-everything. Rear monopod, cheeckpiece, buttplate, this thing does everything but brew your coffee.

You can see the expanding head of the Blaser collet bolt.

Here you see the justification for a monopod; it creates a tripod-mounted shooting platform.

The modern sniper rifle customarily has a bipod on it, as the whole point of the exercise is to shoot precisely and accurately.

use either hand to press the button. Of course, those accustomed to slapping the left-side lever with their left hand will never notice the one on the right. Which is a shame, as you can use your trigger finger to drop the bolt. Especially when shooting from the bench, I found it a lot easier to just angle my trigger finger up and press the tab, than to press with the left hand, and then have to re-settle the rifle in the bags.

For my testing, I did most of my range work with the 20-inch version and my class work with the 16-inch version.

Inside, the 20-inch version has an adjustable Geissele trigger. The other models have either a non-adjustable Geissele, or tuned mil-spec triggers. Geissele has not only designed a fabulous trigger, but they have figured a way for our military to have a match, select-fire trigger. This one, alas, comes semi-only, courtesy the Hughes Amendment to FOPA '86. Still, the Geissele trigger is clean, crisp, and a joy to use.

On the back end is a Magpul PRS, their sniper stock with adjustments for length of pull, comb height and a special rail on the bottom to attach a monopod.

The handguard is the LWRCI ARM-R™ forearm, a low-profile free-float tube, with regularly spaced drilled and tapped holes on the bottom and sides. If you want a bit or more of rail in some section, you simply bolt on the length rail you need (rails and screws provided) at the location you need. If you're handy with tools, you can even measure and cut a longer rail to a shorter length, for just the gear you want on, and no more. It's not only adaptable and customizable but lighter, too. The smaller-diameter tube that results from not having permanent rails makes the rifle very handy. Had LWRCI not made the forearm this way, the result might well have been something so bulky you'd need NBA-sized hands to grab it.

Inside the forearm is a 20-inch heavy contour, cold rotary-forged, Nicorr treated barrel, chambered in 7.62 NATO. The twist is 1:10, and on the end is a .308-sized A2 flash hider. Backing it all up is an LWRCI-upgraded bolt, and what drives it is the LWRCI short-stroke piston system, proportioned for, and beefed up to withstand, .308 power. The LWRCI piston system has a four-position gas adjustment bolt with which you can set the gas for normal, more (adverse conditions), less (using a suppressor), or none (no-cycle suppressor work) at your discretion.

The LWRCI REPR comes with a Magpul 7.62 magazine, which is one of the competing "AR-10" magazine designs. Derived from, and compatible with, the original AR-10 and the M-110 rifle currently used in some branches of the armed forces, the Magpul holds 20 rounds of big-bore goodness. More, you ask? Let's get real. I have 30-round .308/7.62NATO magazines for some other rifles. Trust me, you do not want to be schlepping something that big around, unless you're feeding something select-fire. Twenty is plenty. However, if you must have more, POF makes a 25-round all-steel magazine that also fits the SR-25 pattern.

The top rail of the receiver and forearm are co-planar and continuous to the end of the forearm. You can mount lots of gear there, perhaps more than you really should. The REPR comes with folding sights, front and rear, marked with LWRCI and their logo. To test the performance of the 20-inch REPR on drills, I mounted an EOTech EXP on top, zeroed it, and proceeded to thrash some close-range targets with some drills. What I found out pretty quickly is that I couldn't choke the REPR, and doing fast drills through a lot of big-bore ammo is something you should be in very good shape to do well. It got tiring, even with the big rifle to soak up recoil. So keep that in mind, the next time you feel that a 5.56 is just too "wimpy" and that life would be better with a .308. It will cost you, in ammo, recoil and weapon weight.

A brief aside, to those looking at the REPR spec chart on their web page, who will no-doubt snort something to the effect "An M14 weighs two pounds less." Yes it does. And it has no provision for mounting lights, lasers or scopes in a rational manner. And, it is longer, less accurate, and hardly user-customizable at all.

As for accuracy, I grabbed a LaRue 30mm mount and decided to test out a relatively new scope here at Gun Abuse Central, a Famous Maker 4-14X44 with a 30mm tube tactical scope. With a large-diameter tube and mil-dot reticle, it works just fine in daylight. (I haven't yet had a chance to test it at night, but that will be coming soon.) If my job description included riding in helicopters to places where I'd be kicking down doors, I'm not so sure I'd be depending on a scope that retails for $150. But, as a scope to get started on learn-ing and using mil-dots and for getting a hang for preci-sion or long-range shooting, it will teach you a lot. And I haven't broken this one yet.

Also, to see how it would hold up (as if I had any doubts) I mounted an Insight ATPIAL, a laser target-ing designator that is half the size of the older mil-spec laser, the PEQ-2/A. It had no problems with recoil, and I'm not sure I could harm it short of attacking it with a ball-peen hammer.

I had a pretty decent selection of .308 ammo to run through the REPR, and I managed to get some impres-sive accuracy results for my efforts. As with any rifle, I'm sure this one will show preferences for one load over another, but that will take someone with a little more trigger time on precision rifles than I have. As it was, the rifle shoots well enough to make me look like a brilliant rifleman, and as I said earlier, that makes it very attractive.

For class use, I hauled the 16-inch barreled one off

A Knight's Armament XM110, built for the US military.

to one of our patrol rifle classes. It worked as expected, flawlessly, and I continued my passing/perfect qual scores string. It also was easy to dump the 300-meter pop-ups, even with iron sights.

You want a semi-auto sniper rifle, this one will do the job, easy.

## SIG Blaser Tactical 2

Now, don't get me wrong. Bolt-action rifles have strengths that can't be easily discounted. Let's take, for example, accuracy. We all know what accuracy is, right? All the shots through one hole at absurd distances. Well, partly right. How would you feel about a rifle that put all its shots not just through a ragged group, but through the same hole, time after time? Great, right? What if, each morning, when you pulled it out of the rack, that point of impact was several inches in some random direction? They'll all go through the same hole, but you don't know where the hole will be. That is an accurate rifle, but not a repeatable one.

Bolt-action rifles, especially ones with free-floated barrels, have not just accuracy, but repeatability. Given

The SIG DMR variant of their 556, introducing itself to the long-range steel.

All three of the LWRCI REPRs shot
up to the skill level of the shooter,
and probably had more in them.

the same ammo lot, they will have the same point of impact, day or night, hot or cold, wet or dry.

One such rifle that I've had a chance to test is the SIG Blaser Tactical 2. It is a bolt-action rifle, plopped into a high-tech polymer stock that free-floats the barrel, and offers cheekpiece, buttplate length of pull and pitch adjustments. If you can't make this one fit you, you're harder to fit than an NBA player. And in case you need fast follow-up shots, while it has a bolt handle on the side, you don't turn and pull, you just pull. It is a straight-pull bolt action, where the bolt head is an expanding collet that locks securely to the barrel extension.

As if that weren't enough, you can have it in four different calibers; .223, .308, .300 Winchester Magnum, and .338 Lapua. Now, at the extreme, with the .338 Lapua and its 27-inch barrel, you have a rifle that starts out at just over 12-1/2 pounds. But, even with the muzzle brake, when you touch off a Lapua round, you'll be glad it is that heavy.

I had an afternoon with one at the SIG plant, and with it I was able (in the .308 version) to shoot a bragging-size target.

A shooting mat does more than keep your uniform clean. It keeps movement and muzzle blast from creating dust. And a puff of dust, at the wrong moment, could be very, very bad.

For a police application, where the distance is short and the timeframe shorter, a handy bolt-action rifle can still work just fine.

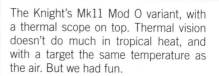

The Knight's Mk11 Mod O variant, with a thermal scope on top. Thermal vision doesn't do much in tropical heat, and with a target the same temperature as the air. But we had fun.

The standard caliber for regular sniper rifles is .308, with the most accurate bullet/load that can be obtained.

One of the DSA-built sniper rifles for the Army tests, built on the FAL.

As the Army requested, the stock adjusts, the cheeckpiece adjusts, and the triggers were very nice.

## SIG DMR

If you have the opportunity as a team leader (LEO or military) to have a school-trained sniper along with you, you have a very useful asset. However, you won't. The next-best thing is to get a really accurate rifle into the hands of the best shooter on your squad or platoon and have him do the medium-range sniping for you. In the military, that job description is Squad Designated Marksman.

A scope on an M16 or M4 is good, but the military has been building purpose-made rifles for the job. SIG makes their 556 Classic in a DMR configuration. It uses, instead of the 16-inch barrel, a 21-inch tube, and the stock is a Magpul PRS stock. The trigger is an en-

hanced single-stage trigger, which means it is built to be cleaner than the already nice SIG 556 trigger, and the forearm is instead of the polymer halves, a railed free-float setup. Well, as much as you can free-float a piston-driven barrel.

With it, I was able to commit wholesale slaughter among one-liter water bottles at 200 yards, and hitting a LaRue steel plate at 600 was so easy it almost became boring. I say "almost" because once I had figured the drop (a 5.56 round, depending on the load, drops 50 to 60 inches out there) I started doing head-shots only.

The rifle was so soft to shoot, and so accurate, that I almost gave in and asked what the special writer's price would be on one.

**Chapter 14**

# Rimfires

'm sure someone is going to ask, "What's so tactical about a rimfire rifle?" In the right circumstances, a lot. There is nothing else out there that will provide you with more shots for less weight. Ammo weight, that is. Other advantages of the rimfire, and they are considerable, include low noise, low recoil, and – if you're willing to do some leg work to find the right combo – often brilliant accuracy.

However, keep in mind that you will not have the hammer of Thor in your hands. No matter how cool or dolled-up it might be, (Quick; bonus points for those who know the name of his hammer. Yes, it has a name.) *[It's "Mjöllnir" –Editor.]*

The .22LR will still and always be a 40-grain bullet at a thousand feet per second, more or less. However, in a whole lot of circumstances, that can be plenty.

I can see two broad circumstances where a .22LR (not a .17 and not a Magnum) would be very, very useful: in training and after TEOTWAWKI (The End Of The World As We Know It).

Training first. When it comes time to teach a new shooter, the dual problems of noise and recoil make learning difficult. A loud firearm triggers the startle reflex sooner, harder and more frequently than a quiet one does. That makes it more difficult to train out the reflex and get to marksmanship. A hard-kicking firearm is just painful, and not a whole lot of people are willing to put up with pain for an end result they are not so sure they need.

Also, a .22LR, especially fed subsonic ammo and fired out of a rifle barrel, will be so quiet that no one will complain. (Except the neighbors who bought a house cheap because it was next to the rifle range, and now complain about the noise.) In fact, you have to be careful, as the low noise will actually lead some people to discount the hazard a firearm can present. For many, low noise means low power, and that can lead to tragic consequences. So, build all the good habits and teach the four rules.

For proper training, it is best if you have an exact duplicate of the big-bore rifle you'll be using. This is easy for some and not so easy for others. While the current trend to ARs has lots and lots of .22LR copies to be had, you'll have to search very hard to find a .22LR trainer FAL. That should not stop you, as any training is good, and you can learn to switch from one rifle to another just by handling and dry-firing. So shoot for trigger control and feedback on the range with a .22LR, and dry-fire your FAL. Once you're confident (or rather, once your student is) then start shooting a few rounds from the FAL or whatever other big-bore rifle you're having them transition to.

The second instance in which a rimfire would come in handy would be the End Times, when what we laughingly call modern civilization has come crashing down around our ears. You'll need to pot something for dinner, but it would be wasteful (both of ammo and target) to "bag" a squirrel with a .308. You'd have to be a brilliant shot to both kill it and leave enough to actually eat. Also, as noted, a .22LR is quiet, and if you take some measures to quiet it still more you could well pass unnoticed. Everything you can do to not get noticed, post-Apocalypse, is good.

The current rage is for .22LR rifles based on, or built like, the AR-15. For those who own an AR, that's great. But for the rest, it takes some searching to find a clone close enough to be a good understudy.

## SIG 522

The 522 is a clone of the 566 Classic, except that it is in .22LR. That said, you know that there is no piston system, as all .22LR rifles are blowbacks. (Well, the self-loading ones, anyway.) There is no need to complicate things more than that, since the rimfire is small enough to be handled and contained by a simple blowback system.

In handling and operation, it works the same. The receiver is the same design of steel stampings, folded and welded, as its big brother. The polymer parts are the same as well. If you aren't careful, and look closely at the ejection port, you could get to the range and find you've grabbed your 522 and your 5.56 magazines, or vice-versa. The magazines are also sturdy, and here SIG again took a look at what was out there and decided they really didn't need to re-invent the wheel.

Instead of some new design, SIG went with the current (and hell for tough) designs that are all either copies of, or made by, Black Dog. The shell of the magazines is an incredibly tough polymer, and there is a .22LR magazine in the middle of it. The magazines will fit in regular AR magazine pouches, and they feel much the same.

Now with an MSRP in the mid-$500 range, it may seem a bit pricey for "just a plinker." Consider it, instead, an understudy to your SIG 556. Each 100 rounds of .22LR you shoot costs you perhaps three dollars. A hundred rounds of 5.56, $30. At over $300 per thousand rounds difference in price, you don't have to do a whole lot of shooting to recoup the investment in your 522.

The SIG 522, being used to hammer down falling steel plates. Small plates, agreed, but still very good practice.

The rimfire clone of a SCAR, not yet available, but looking very good.

Except for the ejection port, hard to tell from the real SCAR.

And the stock even folds, as the centerfire models do.

## A SCAR .22

I had a chance to handle a copy of the SCAR, but not one made by FNH-USA. Planned to be imported by Austrian Sporting Arms, it is a dead copy of the SCAR-L, the 5.56 version. But, chambered in .22LR, it should be a lot less expensive and have the same ammunition economy as the SIG 522 mentioned above.

It is not at the moment imported, but it is such a bit of eye-candy that I just had to include it.

# Chapter 15

# Slings and Such

Yes, reloading your rifle is a good thing, but sometimes you really need a blaster in your hands, faster than you can top off your rifle. And, despite the best efforts, there will be times when your rifle is out of reach. Perhaps only a step, but that step may be more than time permits.

That is why you have a handgun on. You do have a handgun on, don't you?

The first thing to consider is just where is it? Belt, shoulder rig, thigh rig, vest mount, where? If at all possible, you should get into the habit of always wearing it in the same place, so you don't have to frisk yourself to find it in an emergency. That, said, transitioning to the handgun also depends on just how you have your rifle slung. There are three methods: single-point, two-point, and three-point sling.

Regardless of which you have, and where your gun is, there are a few basics you have to follow.

First: Safety On! Yes, you may well have need of your handgun because your rifle is empty or it is jammed to the point where getting it working will take too long. You still need to get into the habit of putting its safety on. You'll be doing a lot of training and practice without a malfunction or running dry, and you do not want your rifle bouncing around, loaded, with its safety off.

Second, you have to get your rifle out of the way, away from the handgun. It does no good to sweep the rifle to the side, only to have it trap your handgun.

## Single-Point

This is where the sling is a self-closed loop and clips to the rifle at just one point, usually somewhere at the rear of the receiver. The big advantage is that you can easily shift from one shoulder to the other and shoot the rifle around the "wrong corner" without sticking too much of yourself out into view. That said, there are some definite downsides to a single-point sling. First of all, you can't just "let it hang." To do so, as above, invites the trigger to be pressed by some errant piece of gear. And, if you do it often enough, you'll catch the handguards, light, laser or front sight assembly right in the shorts.

It is important to get the rifle off to the side. With it out of the way, draw your handgun.

## Two-Point

This is the front and rear mounted sling, usually mounted on the side of the rifle rather than at the bottom. It's not your basic leather strap for shoulder carry and it's certainly not a target sling to wrap your arm in. There are two ways to carry/wear this sling. One is to stick your support arm and head through it; the other to stick your shooting arm and head through it.

If you do the support/arm method, when you let go of the rifle it will point down and to the side. This method also allows for some security in muzzle control. The "down and to the side" method also pins the rifle across your chest.

The shooting arm/head method makes the rifle at rest hang horizontally. If you are all by yourself, this will work fine. But if you have anyone else around, you have to be very careful how and where you stand, as the muzzle is pointing directly to the side. To draw, you'll have to not only push the rifle to the side, but drag the sling along, to get the rifle over far enough to get it out of the way. The support/head sling option gets the muzzle down, at an angle, and pretty much keeps it there. The shooting/head option leaves it hanging horizontally, and you will not make any friends that way.

Also, the horizontal option has another downside: doors and corners. With the muzzle sticking out a foot or so, every door you go through, every corner you pass, is another opportunity for the muzzle to catch, whack, make noise and be damaged.

### Three-Point

The classic three-point sling is the one you often see on the HK MP5, where you have a two-point base and a one-point slider. The idea is to have the best of both worlds: enough movement to let you get the stock to your other shoulder but have it hang vertically.

The problem with the three-points is that they are all complicated. If you were to hand a three-point sling to a dozen shooters and have them install and wear the rifle with that sling, no instructions, you'd probably see three or four variations. Which one would be right? Probably the one the fewest of them were using.

### Drawing

OK, you've gotten the rifle out of the way. If you haven't/hadn't, the draw stroke would be interrupted by the handgun crashing into the rifle, usually the magazine. Not only is that not "high-speed/low-drag," it's also going to slow down your draw, disturb your ability to deal with the problem at hand, and have your nickname changed to "Billiard Boy" (since your draw is always a three-bank shot).

Once the rifle is out of the way, your draw is like any other: get a secure grip, draw up, punch out, and align the sights. Since you are restraining your rifle, you may well be shooting one-handed. Even if you are not, you'll have your support hand catch up later than it probably does, so get used to one-handed shooting.

Here we have two items of interest: 1Lt. Worthington has a vest-mounted holster and a single-point sling. DoD photo by Spc. Kristina Gupton, U.S. Army.

The rifle goes click, and there is no time to reload.

Press it farther back, as you go for your handgun.

Swing it to the side, and out of the way.

If you have a hunk of gear on the side, something you can hang the rifle over, or you have a restraining device, you can secure your rifle after a few handgun shots, deal with the problem, then proceed.

A lot of SWAT officers, and military folks who deal with non-shooting situations, have some sort of securing gizmo. The simplest one I've seen is simply a length of bungee cord, duct-taped to the web gear. Why? OK, let's assume that you're on an entry team. The team busts in, and everyone sticks their hands up. No one needs to be shot. How are you going to apply the handcuffs, if you're holding a rifle? Handcuffs are not a one-handed affair. Leaving your rifle hanging is an invitation for someone to grab it.

Or let's say you have to apply emergency medical treatment to someone. You don't want your rifle hanging in the way, dragging your laser targeting indicator across the wound, getting the laser bloody and the wound infected. So you need to get the rifle out of the way, even/or especially when you aren't going to the handgun. A duct-taped bungee does the job as well as anything else, even if it does look like a low-end "field expedient," which is exactly what it is.

The rest is standard handgun technique.

Swing the rifle out to the side and back, to clear the holster.

Starting again, we get he click, indicating a pressing need for more bullets.

The movement to get past the holster is longer (and slower) than going to the offside.

Rifle down, grasp the pistol.

Then up and complete the handgun-only portion of your problem-solving solution.

Clear the holster, and keep your off hand out of the way as you complete the draw.

Unless you secure it, the rifle is going to swing on the sling, which might be a problem.

## Thigh Rigs

Thigh rigs were high fashion a short while ago. They still retain a certain panache, a high-speed/low-drag swagger to them. Care to hazard a guess what boosted their popularity? Navy SEALS. Once the SEALS started being seen with them, that was it. The masses had to have them.

Quiz time! Why do the SEALS use thigh rigs? Bueller? Bueller? Because SEALS spend a lot of time swimming. Yes, you knew that. But, have you ever scuba-dived? The scuba gear is absolutely unforgiving of compromise. If you have scuba gear on, you cannot put something else where it is. And you cannot move the scuba gear. It is where it is, and anything else has to go someplace else.

By the time a swimmer has the straps for the tanks, the weight belt and the other dive gear secured around their middle, there is no room/place for a holster. Or the belt to hold it. So, the holster went down on the thigh. "Great," you say "So what about when they aren't swimming?" Rule number one, when wearing weapons and going deliberately into harm's way: You place something, and you leave it. No moving holsters around, depending on if you are diving or not. Once on the thigh, the holster stays there, even if a SEAL (or any smart student of combat) finds himself a hundred miles from the nearest potential scuba opportunity.

Now, clearly, if a SEAL or other SpecOps guy draws an assignment that simply doesn't permit a thigh rig, he'll wear it where it has to be worn. And, if he's smart, he'll spend a lot of time practicing to draw from the new location.

Of course, once down on the thigh, the draw stroke is the same, you just have to condition yourself to grabbing thigh instead of belt.

## Bullpups

Now, as I've mentioned elsewhere, bullpups bring problems along with advantages. (Everything does, or we wouldn't have so many pesky choices to make.) However, when it comes to drawing the handgun, a bullpup is like any other rifle: you have to get it out of the way. Being (generally) shorter, the bullpup will be easier to get clear, but you still have to do it.

## Vest-Mounted

The lessons learned in Iraq included some very interesting ones. The first concerned the number of combatants (our side) who were riding around in vehicles.

Get the rifle out of the way, or your handgun will hit it.

You might even have the handgun knocked out of your hand.

Practicing with their sidearms, Marines work out of thigh rigs. Of particular note is the gentleman in the middle, using a 1911 instead of an M9. USMC photo by Lance Cpl. George J. Papastrat.

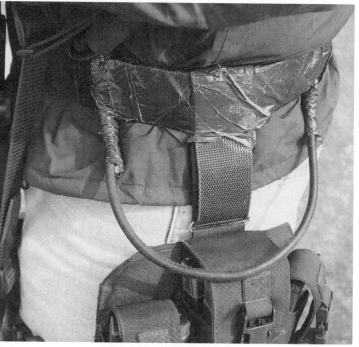

A simple rig like a section of bungee cord duct-taped to your gear will suffice to hold your rifle.

Here you see the rifle, stuffed through the loop, and now out of the way for other action.

A vest-mount draw begins by getting both the rifle and the sling out of the way.

Grasp the pistol, but keep your other arm out of the way.

Once the muzzle clears your important parts, then your support hand can catch up.

Not a big deal, you say? Lots of mechanized infantry rode in Germany, training for the Soviet onslaught. Yes, but they rode inside vehicles carrying them, basically in "battle taxis." In Iraq, they were in Humvees, and later, up-armored Humvees, all working as gunners, ready to repel boarders and shoot from the truck.

In a vehicle, a rifle in a rack or a handgun in a belt holster is not of much use. Enter the vest-mounted holster. Right-handed for those on the driver's side, and left-handed (although an M4 muzzle out of the window works wonders) for those on the passenger side, a vest-mounted holster gets the pistol (typically a Beretta M9) up away from the belt and the gear and the seatbelt.

However, as with all things, the advantages bring disadvantages. The primary one here is that a vest-mounted holster has the muzzle pointing in the direction of your other arm. When you go to get the rifle out of the way, you have to move it further.

You have to move it farther for two reasons: one, to clear the holster lashed to your chest; and two, to get your arm clear of the muzzle as you draw.

## A Reason To Be Different

Now, in all this discussion of getting to the handgun, I've been emphasizing the need to get the rifle out of the way. There is one instance where you do not want to get it out of the way: when you need a light, that is, if you have a light on your rifle, no light on your handgun, and it is dark and your rifle has stopped working. Then, you want to keep the rifle pointed in the direction you will be shooting. You hold the rifle with one hand and draw with the other.

This is not easy. I had one suggestion, once, of putting the rifle under your arm. First of all, it is a bulky and heavy object to keep clamped under your arm. And second, the sling prevents it. Most slings will strangle you before you can get the rifle tucked under your arm.

So, instead, hold the rifle under the forearm, controlling direction and light, and draw and shoot. Awkward? Yes, but everything else is worse. Not having a light on your handgun has gotten you into this predicament, and maybe next time you'll have a sidearm with a light on it. Or a rifle that keeps working.

Not all actions that require getting the rifle out of the way also require using a handgun. Here, I get to play the casualty, and the team members try to keep their muzzles out of the mud and off me.

PO2 Kowall, readying his vehicle for convoy duty in Afghanistan, has his M9 in a vest-mounted holster. DoD photo by Master Sgt. Demetrius Lester, U.S. Air Force.

# Reloading

Not reloading ammo, but reloading rifles. As my friend John Farnam quips, often as not "the leading cause of rifle malfunction is running out of ammo." You run out, you have to get more. Now, sometimes that "getting more" is so imperative, so time-sensitive, that "getting more" means letting go of the empty firearm you're holding, grabbing another loaded one instead of stuffing a fresh supply of noise-makers into the blaster you're holding.

And, for those who will quibble if I don't point it out, what I'm demonstrating and discussing is always done in the context of cover, concealment and observation. You do not simply stand still, in the open, and perform a reload of any kind. Not speed, not tactical, not existential. Unless you are in the middle of nowhere, with no cover to be had at all (and just how did you arrive there, anyway?) the first thing to do when you need to reload is get behind something solid. Keep watching your surroundings, reload and get back to business as quickly as you can.

In some instances, our troops had to learn this lesson all over again in Iraq. The famous Newhall Incident in Southern California in the early 1970s, taught that lesson to law enforcement. However, what one group knows, another does not, and if there is no communication between them, no chance to learn the easy way. So, when we are discussing reloads, always assume that I have begun each part of it under the assumption that you are behind cover, keeping your head up and watching (as much as you can, without getting shot), ready to fight.

First of all, keep in mind that while there are commonly considered to be two types or kinds of reloads, tactical and speed, there really aren't. If you have run out, you have no idea of just how much time you may or may not have until you need to fire again, if you need to fire at all. However, doing speed reloads all the time will soon run your supply of magazines down to none, and then what will you do?

Now, in a military context I can see being solicitous of one's magazines. You may be hours of firefight, or days of patrol, away from a reliable resupply of spare magazines. So, it makes sense any time you feel you have a chance to save a known and reliable magazine, that you do so. Just keep in mind that you may be in the middle of a "tactical" reload when you need to shoot again, and the best thing you can have done for that time is practiced the speed reload. Drop that empty, stuff another loaded magazine in, and get to work.

In a law enforcement or non-sworn defensive situation, the idea that you might blast through your ready supply of loaded magazines and need to reload them is well beyond extraordinary. Thinking in those terms is going well into the zombie apocalypse zone, and beyond our purview here. If you have two or three spare magazines, you will be set for 99.99% of all recorded gunfights.

How you reload? Muzzle-up or not? Let's see.

The beginning of a tactical reload. You have a chance; you reload before you need to.

Grab the magazine, press the release, and pull.

Bring the rifle down.

When the magazine comes free…

. . .you put it in whatever carrier you have for partial magazines.

Grab a fresh magazine, one with lots of bullets in it.

## Muzzle-Up

The muzzle-up method (and I'll be using an AR for this example, because it was developed around that rifle) is simple: you pull the trigger and nothing happens. Unshoulder the rifle and drop the butt down, while at the same time turning the ejection port of the rifle towards you. This is so you can see what's going on. If it is a malfunction, correct it. If you're empty, reload it. Press the magazine button, and as you hold it down, snap the rifle back toward alignment, and then past it. This does two things: it propels the empty magazine out of the rifle, and it turns the magazine well towards the left hand. (All reloading procedures have been developed with right-handed shooters in mind. Lefties, you'll have to adapt. But then, you always have to, anyway. Sorry about that, I didn't make the rules.) While you do this, you reach down with your left hand to grab the next magazine.

Bring it up to the mag well, line the spine of the mag up with the mag well, and once it is nicely meshed, shove it home. Slide your hand up to the receiver, slap or press the bolt hold-open to close the bolt, bring the muzzle down on-target, and get back to work.

The method is popular with the military, primarily due to keeping the muzzle up and out of the way. Another variant is to keep the muzzle on-target, press the mag button, and as an assist, slide the left hand back and snatch the magazine down out of the receiver. (It is probably already falling, but why not help it on its way anyway?)

Another reason it is popular is from competition. Unbeknownst to a lot of military folks these days, the "cool, high-speed" techniques that they learn in the military that they use in sandy areas, were taught to their instructors (or their instructor's instructors) years ago by high-speed low-drag IPSC competitors. I've been seeing it a bit now, since we have veterans who are putting out a shingle as a tactical firearms instructor: I've had the relatively amusing experience of being taught a "military, combat-proven" technique, one that I watched the IPSC Grandmasters of 20 years ago develop. (Imagine the horror of the mall ninjas and gun shop commandos, if they could grasp the irony.)

A variant of these is to actually raise the rifle as you go to reload, bringing the mag well right into your direct line of vision, exactly as in the handgun reload from competition. The competition application is simple: it gets the magazine well up into your field of vision, and also keeps you looking outwards, not down. It mimicks

Press the magazine home.

Bring the rifle back up, ready to shoot.

If the bolt is locked back (or even if it isn't) slap the bolt hold-open button. If it was open, it will close. If it was closed, it won't care.

On a speed reload, you go for the next magazine as you hit the magazine release button.

Let the old magazine fall free and grab the new one as quickly as possible.

The high reload begins with the click instead of a bang.

Reload as quickly as you can. (And get behind cover, if you can.)

Turn the rifle to observe the ejection port. If a malfunction, deal with it. If empty, reload.

If doing a high reload, competition-style, lift the rifle up so the magazine well is in your line of sight.

The muzzle-level method has you clamping the buttstock between your arm and body, to keep it under control.

Push the magazine in, and try to pull it out.

With the rifle secured, grab the next magazine.

As you raise the rifle, slap the bolt hold-open.

Get the magazine up to the rifle, and index the mag to the well.

Slapping the bolt catch to close the bolt, chambering a round.

Push the magazine home, and then try to pull it out. If it stays, you're good, get to....

Slap the bolt hold-open as you raise the rifle.

It will take practice, but keep your eyes up, and scanning your surroundings, while reloading.

Bullpups call for some gymnastics in reloading.

Two mistakes here: the first is not supporting the rifle and allowing it to 'float' in space. The other is in not watching the surroundings.

the handgun reload, where the gun is kept high, and you look "through" the gun as you reload.

The drawbacks to this technique are several: The muzzle-high position "flags" you for anyone down-range. If you are behind cover, a muzzle sticking up lets people know where you are, and more importantly, when they see the muzzle dip, they know you're done reloading, and will be popping out somewhere, ready to shoot again. Also, it takes a certain amount of hand/arm strength to keep the rifle pointed up, while you grab a spare magazine and reload.

## Muzzle Level

Keep the muzzle level or a bit downwards-pointing. Press the mag button and let the mag fall free. Assist it if it hesitates. Bring the butt down and clamp it under your arm. Grab the next magazines line it up, and press it home. As you raise the rifle, press or slap the bolt hold-open and close the bolt.

The advantages of this method are strength; the rifle is not going to move with it clamped under your arm. The drawback is that with the rifle down, your eyes will have to, at some point at the very least flock down to get the mag in. You risk having your head down when you should be looking around.

You can turn the rifle inward and use your support hand to reload a bullpup.

## AK Variant

To reload with an AK (or FAL or M14), you have to modify things a bit. The magazine release on the AK is not a button but a paddle behind the magazine. Also, the AK magazine does not ride straight up to lock; you have to rock it into place. So, to get the old magazine out, you have to "pinch" the magazine. That is, grab it with your thumb, pressing the magazine catch paddle, and then rock it forward. You can then let go when it comes free, launching it out into space. Or you can hold on to it and stash it away.

An alternative is to grab the next magazine first, and when you bring it up to the rifle, use the magazine (or if your hands are big enough, that thumb) to press the paddle and launch the magazine.

Then, hook the front latch of the magazine into the receiver and pivot it back until it latches.

Regardless of which you use, you next have to rotate the rifle again, to bring the ejection port over to your side, reach over, and work the charging handle. Unlike the AR, the AK does not lock open, and you have to work the bolt to get a new round into the chamber.

As much as it pains me to say it, the procedure for the M14/M1A and the FAL are exactly the same as for the AK. The M14/M1A requires you to reach over to work the charging handle. Yes, the bolt locks open, but the bolt lock button is so small that trying to work it to close the bolt is just a miserable task. It is far better to reach over, yank the handle, and let go. The FAL has a bolt release on the bottom, near the magazine itself. But the area is littered with small levers and parts, and trying to find the right one, under stress, is again a miserable task. Unless you've trained extensively and almost exclusively with an FAL, you're better off working the charging handle. Ditto the Mini-14.

## Reloading Mistakes

You can always do it smoother or fster.

The first reloading mistake is in not securing the rifle. If you just hold it out in space, not letting it touch you anywhere but the pistol grip, reloading will be a miserable experience. The reasons some people do it this way (at least until they learn how un-fun it is) is to see things. They want a good, clear view of the maga-

Or you can turn it the other way, using your firing hand.

Either way you do it, you'll have to practice, and you'll have to set up your gear so you can reach the magazines you'll need.

zine well as they insert the magazine. You can see well enough when the rifle is clamped down, and your seeing things better is not helped by a free-floating rifle.

The second comes to us, as so many un-tactical and un-helpful techniques do, from Hollywood. This is the "slap it home" reload. When you reload, regardless of the method you use, you should do it the simple and effective way: push-pull.

Push the magazine into the rifle until it clicks in place. Do not let go. Try to pull it free. If it does pull free, you clearly didn't have it locked in place and can try again. If it does not pull free, it is locked in place, and you need to get on with your work.

Why is slapping bad? Wouldn't it make sure the magazine is locked in place? To quote Cassius, in Shakespeare's *Julius Caesar*: "The problem, dear Brutus, lies not in our stars, but in ourselves." The problem is not in the locking, but what goes on before or after.

If you subscribe to the slap method and your magazine is not locked, it will fall out. I have, more than once, seen someone try to slap a magazine in place, only to have it fall free before they could hit it. Not only does this call for a points deduction from your man-card, but it drops your re-supply of ammo in the dirt, dust, mud or water. Second, and far worse, is a situation I've also seen more than once: your bolt is locked back. You insert a magazine, and then slap it. The bounce causes the top round in the magazine to pop free. When the bolt goes forward, it tries to both chamber the loose round, and also strip and chamber the next round in the magazine, the one which, because of the slap, has been promoted to first. Since two objects cannot occupy the same location, the result is a wedged jam of epic proportions. This is ugly, gets more points deducted, and makes things really slow.

However, there's an even uglier reloading dance that usually goes like this: the shooter, who is usually right-handed, runs out of ammo and needs more. He lets go of the rifle with his support hand and reaches for the next magazine. His left hand searches, and then he realizes that the next magazine is in a right-hand pocket. So, he re-grabs the rifle with the left hand, grabs the ammo with the right, inserts the magazine with his right, then re-grabs the rifle with the right hand, lets go with the left, works the charging handle or bolt release, and then re-grabs with the left. A juggler couldn't have switched hands more often.

If you are right-handed, wear your spare ammo on the left, and reload with the left.

# Conclusion

So, what have we learned here? First, that despite the current white-hot interest in the AR-15, there is a whole world of non-ARs out there. I wish I could have had more for you, but even for one who has so determinedly collected firearms through the years, I have gaps in the rack. There are some I had a chance to acquire, and for reasons now forgotten, passed on, real peaches like the Beretta AR-70, BM-59 and BM-62, all of which were offered to us at the shop at moments when I found myself momentarily unable to swing the deal.

Or the original Steyr AUG, and the Sig Stg90 (both in semi-auto guise) that I passed on, because "magazines are too hard to find." I look back and could kick myself, because even if magazines were hard to find, they had enough with them in the prospective deals. It wasn't like I was going to have to deal with the coming zombie apocalypse with those rifles and their three magazines each, right? (Heck, when those deals were in front of me, no one was even thinking in terms of post-ZA scenarios.)

Then there is the Belgian FNC, and the Browning-marked FAL that I passed on, the FNC because I was too busy learning the intricacies of the AR, and the FAL because I wasn't all that interested in .308s there and then. The various Valmets that passed by, the HK 93 & 91, three different Galils, and I just can't go on. It is too depressing.

The lesson here is simple: unlike horses, motor-driven conveyances and other hobbies, firearms do not consume ammo unless you want them to. A horse has to be fed, watered, shoveled, exercised, and get regular visits from the vet, regardless. A boat has to be scraped and painted; cars, trucks and motorcycles need regular attention; and an airplane practically needs an Italian sports-car level of maintenance unless you want your friends and relatives to discover all the details of your will.

Cleaned and oiled, a rifle in the rack does not ask anything of you at all. If you do not shoot it, your skills get rusty, but the rifle does not depreciate from wear.

So, if something you've always wanted comes by, and you can afford it, buy it. If you take care of it, you'll probably be able to sell it for close to what you paid for it. One of the least-painful, albeit most difficult lessons to learn, are those learned by watching someone else. Learn from me; don't regret passing by a deal. Go buy that tactical rifle you've wanted.